The History of
CASTILLO DE SAN MARCOS

Text and Illustrations from *The Building of Castillo de San Marcos* by Luis Rafael Arana and Albert Manucy.
Additional text by Jay Humphreys, layout and design by Henry Hird.

National Park Service

CONTENTS

Steve Garris

Seen from the air, the symmetry and simplicity of the Castillo reflect its efficiency as a defensible fort. Its location on the bay shore commanded land and water approaches to St. Augustine.

Edited & Published by Historic Print & Map Co., St. Augustine, Florida. Text and some illustrations used with permission by Eastern National. ISBN 978-0-9729463-3-9

© 2005 Historic Print & Map Company   www.historicprint.com   *Learn more St. Augustine history at* **augustine.com**

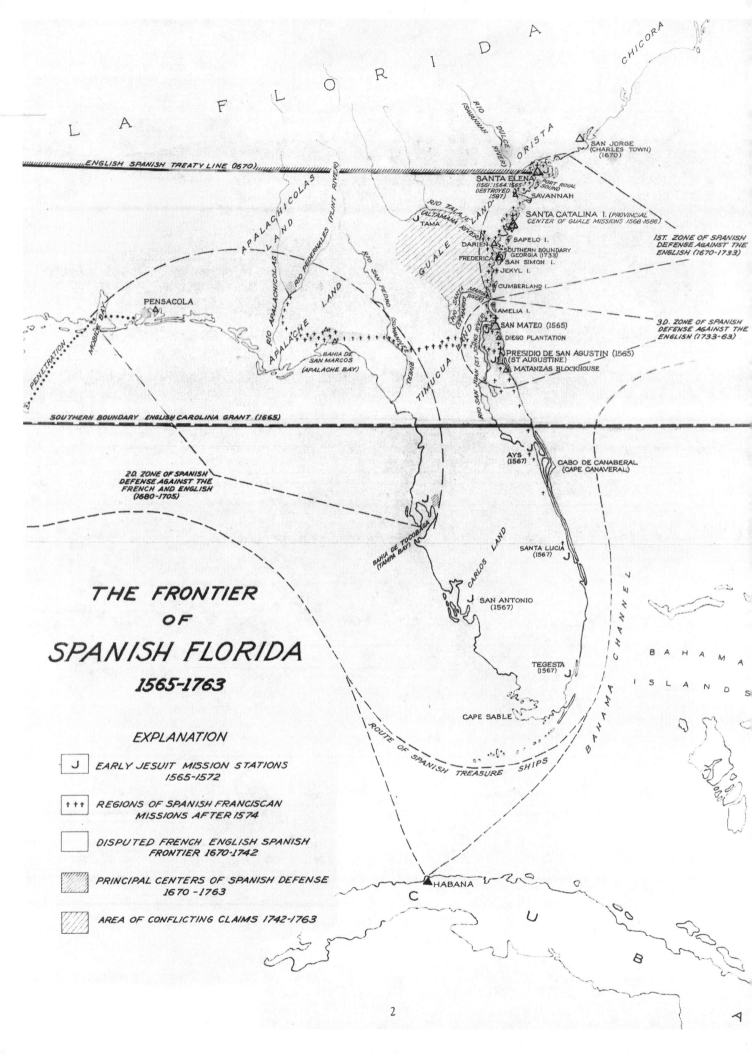

THE FRONTIER
OF
SPANISH FLORIDA
1565-1763

EXPLANATION

J EARLY JESUIT MISSION STATIONS
   1565-1572

+++ REGIONS OF SPANISH FRANCISCAN
     MISSIONS AFTER 1574

     DISPUTED FRENCH ENGLISH SPANISH
     FRONTIER 1670-1742

     PRINCIPAL CENTERS OF SPANISH DEFENSE
     1670 -1763

     AREA OF CONFLICTING CLAIMS 1742-1763

L A   F L O R I D A

CHICORA

ORISTA

SAN JORGE
(CHARLES TOWN)
(1670)

ENGLISH SPANISH TREATY LINE (1670)

SANTA ELENA
(1561-1564-1565-
DESTROYED
1587)

PORT ROYAL SOUND

SAVANNAH

SANTA CATALINA I. (PROVINCIAL
CENTER OF GUALE MISSIONS 1568-1686)

TAMA

SAPELO I.

1ST. ZONE OF SPANISH
DEFENSE AGAINST THE
ENGLISH (1670-1733)

DARIEN

SOUTHERN BOUNDARY
GEORGIA (1733)

FREDERICA

SAN SIMON I.

JEKYL I.

CUMBERLAND I.

AMELIA I.

3D. ZONE OF SPANISH
DEFENSE AGAINST THE
ENGLISH (1733-63)

APALACHICOLAS
LAND

RIO DULCE
(SAVANNAH RIVER)

RIO TALAJE
(ALTAMAHA RIVER)

GUALE

RIO APALACHICOLAS (FLINT RIVER)

RIO PEDERNALES

RIO SAN PEDRO

RIO SANTA
MARIA

RIO SAN JUAN (ST. JOHNS RIVER)

PENSACOLA

APALACHE
LAND

SAN MATEO (1565)

DIEGO PLANTATION

BAHIA DE
SAN MARCOS
(APALACHE BAY)

RIO SUWANEE
(SUWANEE RIVER)

TIMUCUA
LAND

PRESIDIO DE SAN AGUSTIN (1565)
(ST AUGUSTINE)

MATANZAS BLOCKHOUSE

MOBILE BAY

PENETRATION

SOUTHERN BOUNDARY ENGLISH CAROLINA GRANT (1665)

AYS
(1567)

CABO DE CANAVERAL
(CAPE CANAVERAL)

2D. ZONE OF SPANISH
DEFENSE AGAINST THE
FRENCH AND ENGLISH
(1680-1705)

SANTA LUCIA
(1567)

BAHIA DE TOCOBAGA
(TAMPA BAY)

CARLOS
LAND

SAN ANTONIO
(1567)

TEGESTA
(1567)

BAHAMA
ISLANDS

BAHAMA CHANNEL

CAPE SABLE

ROUTE OF SPANISH TREASURE SHIPS

HABANA

C   U   B   A

In the confused dark, the pirates seemed everywhere. They destroyed the weapons in the guardhouse and went on to the government house. Shouting, cursing, they scattered through the narrow streets and seized or shot frightened, half-naked, bewildered people who erupted out of the houses.

Florida and the Pirates

On May 28, 1668, a ship hove to and anchored off St. Augustine harbor. It was a vessel from Veracruz, bringing flour from Nueva España (México) to feed the soldiers and their families in Spanish Florida.

In the town, the drum called the garrison—120 men—to the alert. A launch went out to recognize the newcomer and put the harbor pilot aboard. As they neared the ship, the crew on the launch hailed the Spaniards lining her gunwale. To the routine questions came the usual answers: Friends from Nueva España—come aboard! Two shots from the launch told the town of the recognition, then the seamen warped her alongside the ship.

In St. Augustine, the people heard the signal shots, and rejoiced. The soldiers racked their arms in the main guardhouse on the town plaza. Tomorrow the supplies would come ashore. As the launch pilot stepped aboard the supply ship, an alien crew swarmed out of hiding and leveled their guns at him and the others. He could do nothing but surrender.

About one o'clock that night, a corporal was out on the bay fishing when he sensed the ominous warning that shattered the serenity of the spring night: many oars were pulling across the water toward town. Desperately the fisherman paddled his little craft toward shore. The pirates, four boatloads of them, chased him hotly. They shot him twice, but he got to the fort anyway. His shouts aroused the guards.

At the main guardhouse, a quarter mile from the fort, the sentries heard the shouting and the gunfire. Then the pirates were upon them, a hundred strong. The handful of guards, being

St. Augustine never really looked like this! The sketch, from an "armchair travel" book of 1670, is the artist's fanciful interpretation of a written description. Mistranslation of the Spanish word "montes" (which can mean either forests or mountains) probably accounts for the background mountains. The faintly oriental aspect may be a carryover of the early concept that the New World was part of the exotic Orient.

both out-numbered and practical, ran for the fort. Governor Francisco de la Guerra rushed out of his house and, with the pirates pounding at his heels, joined the guard in the race for the fort. Behind its rotten wooden walls with 33 men, somehow he beat off several assaults. But in the darkness the firefly glow of the matchcord that each arquebusier carried was an inviting target for the enemy.

In the confused dark, the pirates seemed everywhere. They destroyed the weapons in the guardhouse and went on to the government house. Shouting, cursing, they scattered through the narrow streets and seized or shot frightened, half-naked, bewildered people who erupted out of the houses.

Sergeant Major Nicolás Ponce de León, the officer responsible for defending the town, was at home, a sick man, greasy with unction of mercury and weak from the "sweatings" prescribed for him. On hearing the din, he roused himself and rushed to the guardhouse, only to find the pirates had been there first. He turned to the urgent task of shepherding his 70 unarmed soldiers and the others, men, women, and children, to the woods. This he did, leaving the pirates in complete possession of the town. By daybreak the little force at the fort had lost five men, but they claimed 11 pirates killed and 19 wounded. Ponce came from the woods and reinforced the fort with his weaponless men. Also with the daylight, two vessels joined the Veracruz ship. One was St. Augustine's own frigate, taken by the raiders near Habana. In her, the pirates had been able to move in Spanish waters without detection. The other was the

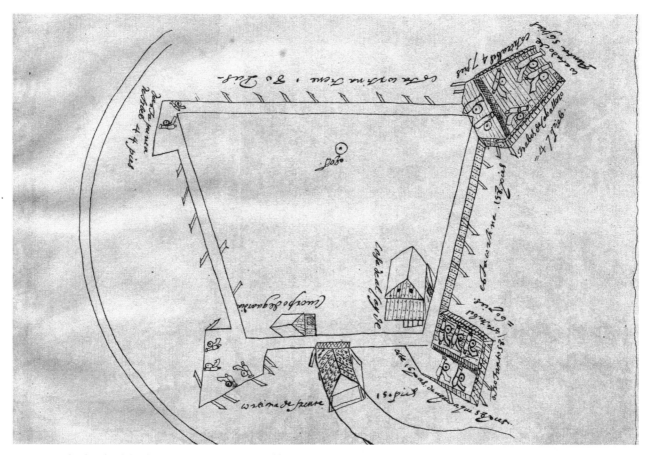

Early sketch of the fort in St. Augustine. Possibly from 1593 according to A Descriptive List of Maps *by Lowery. Original manuscript in Archives of the Indies. Photostat from the Library of Congress*

pirates' own craft. All three sailed into the bay, passed the cannon fire of the fort, and anchored just out of range.

Although their attacks on the fort had failed, the pirates systematically sacked the town. No structure was neglected, from humble thatched dwelling to royal storehouse, hospital, and church. True, the things carried off were but worth a few thousands pesos (pieces-of-eight), for the town was very poor. The booty went aboard the pirate vessel and the ship from Veracruz.

That afternoon, the governor sent out a sortie from the fort, but the leaders were wounded and the party retired. After 20 hours ashore, however, the pirates were ready to leave anyway, and their last boat soon pulled away. Behind them, they left a grief-wracked people 60 of the little community were dead.

But with the tears came prayers of thanksgiving, for the pirates did not hoist anchor until they had ransomed their

prisoners—about 70 men, women, and children—for water, meat and firewood. At the last minute they refused to let the Indians go, claiming that the governor of Jamaica told them to keep all Indians, blacks and mulattoes as slaves, even if they were Spanish freemen. Finally on June 5 the raiders headed out to sea, well enough amused as once again they passed the thunder of the useless guns in the old wooden fort.

The ransomed prisoners could explain the daring raid. It went back to an insult which Governor Guerra, presumably abetted by female friends, had dealt to a Frenchman, one Pedro Piques, who served the presidio as surgeon. Guerra had slapped the surgeon's face and fired him. The disgruntled Frenchman was bound for Habana aboard the St. Augustine frigate when it was captured by the pirates. He must have seen a chance for revenge on Guerra, suggested the raid on St. Augustine, and helped the pirates work out a plan.

This was not the only news. The prisoners identified the invaders as Englishmen. Furthermore, the enemy had carefully sounded the inlet, taken its latitude, and noted the landmarks. They intended to come back and seize the fort and make it a base of operations. Otherwise they would have burned the town.

In Spanish eyes, the sack of St. Augustine was far more than a pirate raid. St. Augustine, though isolated and small, was the keystone in the defense of Florida. And Florida was important, not as a land rich in natural resources, but as a way station on Spain's great commercial route. Each year, galleons bearing the proud Iberian banners drove past the coral keys and surf-pounded beaches of Florida, following the Gulf Stream on their way to Cadiz. In these galleons were millions of ducats worth of gold and silver from the mines of Peru and México, and all of Europe knew it.

The trouble began the year after Magellan's ship encircled the world in 1522: Hernando Cortes dispatched a shipload of treasure from conquered México, but the loot never reached the Spanish court. Instead, a French corsair took it to Francis I. That incident opened a new age in the profitable profession of piracy. Daring adventurers of all nationalities sailed westward. Many found shelter in the West Indies.

Florida's position on the life line connecting Spain with her colonies gave this sandy peninsula certain strategic importance. Spain knew that Florida must be defended to prevent enemies from using the harbors as havens from which they could spread their sails against Spanish commerce. Besides, Florida's lee shores and deadly reefs combined with hurricanes in the narrow Bahama Channel to wreck many a good ship. Scores of mariners were cast ashore on the inhospitable coast. Florida had to be made safe for them, as well as unsafe for enemies.

It was a sizable defense problem. The French triggered the solution in 1564 with Fort Caroline, a colony named for their teenage King Charles, near the mouth of Florida's St. Johns

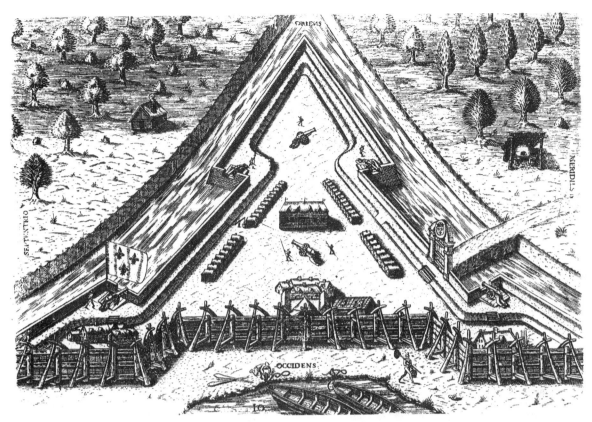

The French built Fort Caroline in 1564, a colony named for King Charles, near the mouth of Florida's St. Johns River.

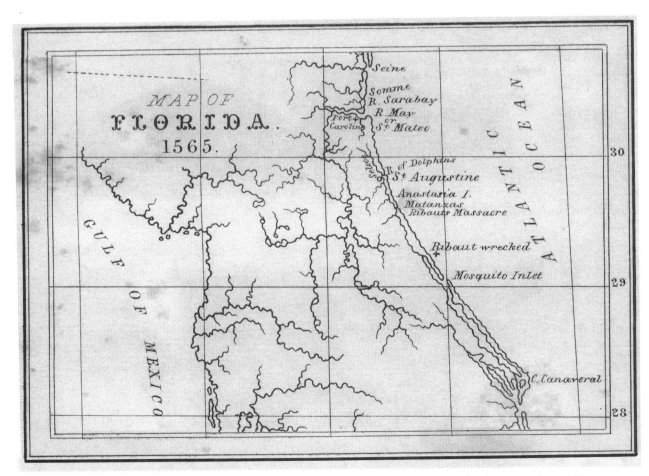

Map from The History & Antiquities of St. Augustine, Florida *by George Fairbanks published in 1858.*

MASSACRE OF THE HUGUENOTS AT FORT CAROLINE.

Laying out of St. Augustine.

River. The French settlement drew Spanish Admiral Pedro Menéndez de Avilés to Florida in 1565. He established the St. Augustine colony and forthwith removed the Frenchmen, some of whom had already begun piratical careers. Now, with this small fortified settlement on one side of the Bahama Channel and growing Habana on the other, Spanish ships could normally pass safely from the ports of Nueva España to those of the Old Country.

Where the sword of Spain went, the cross went also. Gradually a system of missions developed in Florida—fingers of civilization reaching far out into the wilderness. The missionaries had to be protected both from hostile aborigine and European, so defense became a dual operation. The unceasing hunt of naval patrols for pirates, storm-wracked vessels, and starving castaways was paralleled on land by fast-marching patrols along the Indian trails or swift-sailing piraguas in the coastal waterways. St. Augustine was the base of operations, and from its very beginning it was protected by fortifications stronger than any others in the Florida province.

A typical early fort was San Juan de Pinos, burned by the English freebooter Francis Drake in 1586. Drake took away its bronze artillery and some 2,000 pounds sterling "by the treasure's value." Such a fort as San Juan consisted of a pine stockade around small buildings for gunpowder storage and quarters. Cannon were mounted atop a broad platform or cavalier, so they could fire over the stockade.

Such forts could be built quickly. But with equal facility could they be destroyed. If Indian

S. AVGVSTINI
PARS EST FLORI=
DÆ LAT. 30 GRAD.

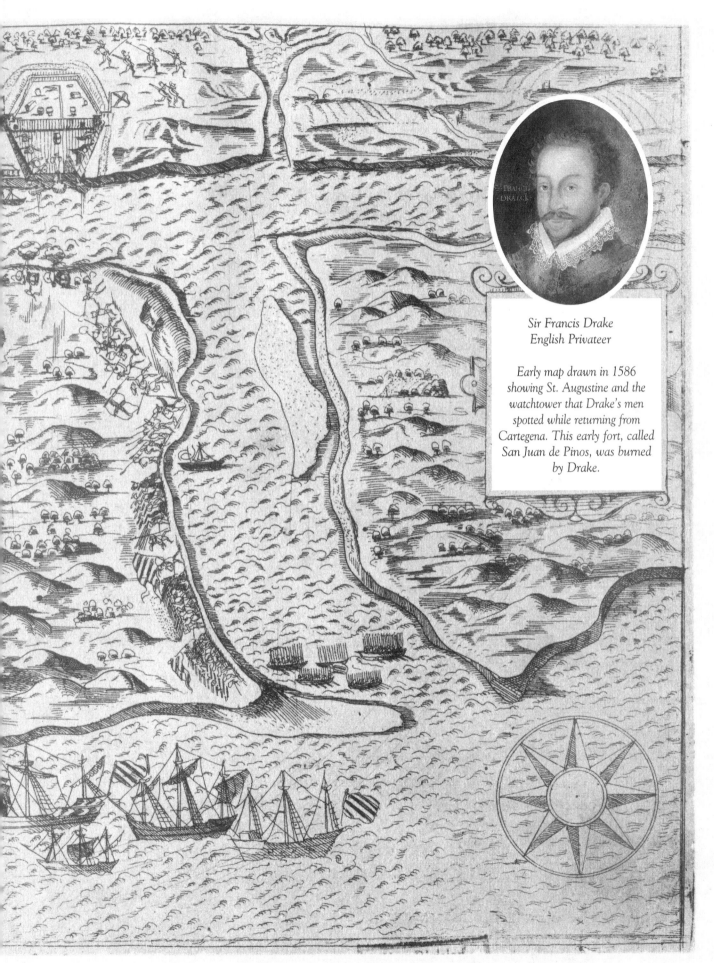

Sir Francis Drake
English Privateer

Early map drawn in 1586
showing St. Augustine and the
watchtower that Drake's men
spotted while returning from
Cartegena. This early fort, called
San Juan de Pinos, was burned
by Drake.

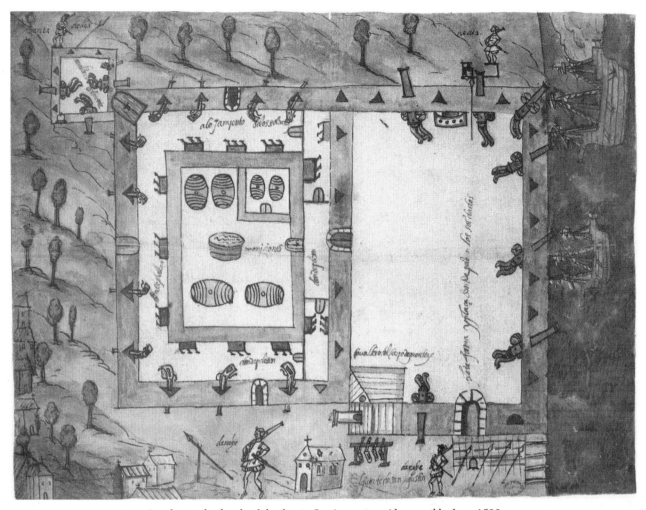

Another early sketch of the fort in St. Augustine. Also possibly from 1593.
Original manuscript in Archives of the Indies, Seville, Spain.

fire arrows or enemy attack or mutinies failed, then hurricanes, time and termites were certain to do the job. During the century before Castillo de San Marcos, nine wooden forts one after another were built at St. Augustine.

Frankly, Spain did not yet see the need for an impregnable fort here. After the English failures at Roanoke in 1586-87, the weakling settlement of Jamestown a few years later did not impress the powerful Council of the Indies at faraway Madrid. Moreover, the Franciscans, by extending the mission frontier deep into Indian lands, put the Spanish stamp of occupation upon a vast territory and seemed a sure means of keeping out rival Europeans. The fallacy in this thinking lay in (1) disparaging the colonizing ability of the Anglo-Saxon and (2) believing that an Indian friendly to Spain would not also befriend England. It turned out that the

English trader, equipped with glittering presents and shrewd promises, was quite able to persuade native customers to desert the strict teachings of the friar and line up with the English.

The 1588 defeat of the powerful Spanish Armada in the English Channel was a dramatic harbinger of things to come. With the Spanish fleet crippled, the way was clear for Britannia's career as mistress of the seas. For England, the 1600's began an era of commercial and colonial expansions. Her great trading companies were active on the coasts of four continents. Powerful English nobles strove for possessions beyond the seas. Jamestown, seemingly an uncertain beginning in North America, was soon followed by the settlements in New England and elsewhere. South from the James River region to the Spanish Florida settlements stretched a vast, rich territory too tempting to ignore, and in

A Spanish Galleon.

The trouble began the year after Magellan's ship encircled the world in 1522: Hernando Cortes dispatched a shipload of treasure from conquered México, but the loot never reached the Spanish court. Instead, a French corsair took it to Francis I. That incident opened a new age in the profitable profession of piracy. Daring adventurers of all nationalities sailed westward. Many found shelter in the West Indies.

Florida's position on the life line connecting Spain with her colonies gave this sandy peninsula certain strategic importance. Spain knew that Florida must be defended to prevent enemies from using the harbors as havens from which they could spread their sails against Spanish commerce. Besides, Florida's lee shores and deadly reefs combined with hurricanes in the narrow Bahama Channel to wreck many a good ship. Scores of mariners were cast ashore on the inhospitable coast. Florida had to be made safe for them, as well as unsafe for enemies.

For protection against corsairs, Spain's outbound vessels traveled in convoy. They picked up the treasure from Cartegena, Panama and Veracruz and gathered together in Habana. They crossed the Atlantic on the Gulf Stream and returned on the west-flowing Equatorial Current.

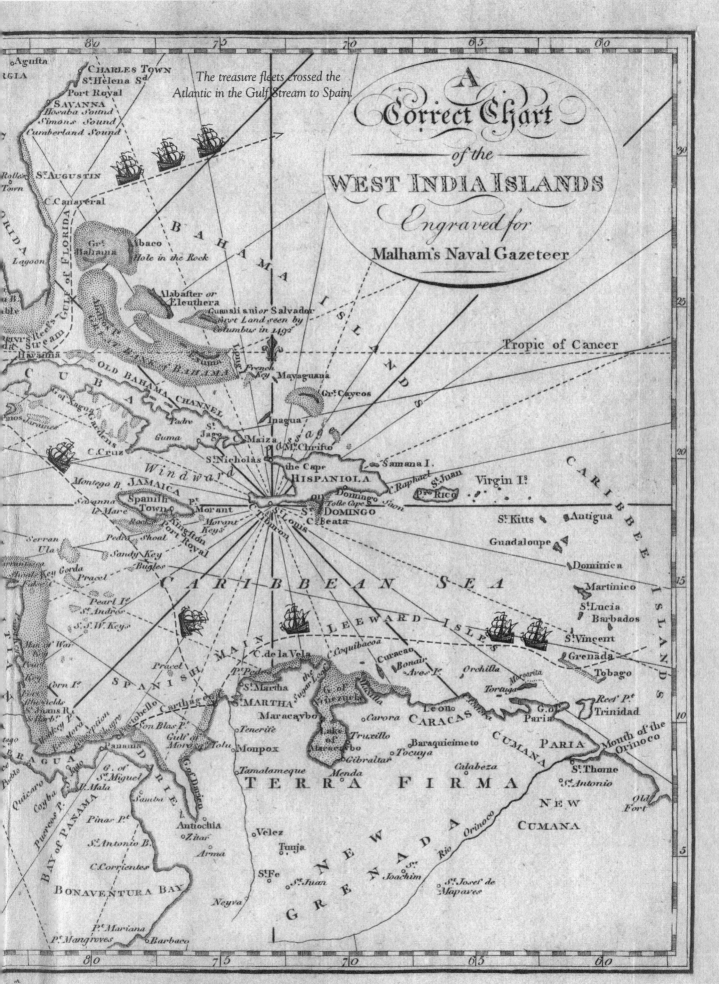

1665 the British crown granted a patent for its occupation. The boundaries of the new colony of Carolina brazenly included some hundred miles or more Spanish-occupied land—even St. Augustine itself! The trend was clear. The fight for Florida was inevitable.

In the middle 1600's at St. Augustine, just south of where the Castillo now stands, there was a wooden fort. It was almost as large as the Castillo. But it was a fort only in name. Its walls were weak with rotted timbers and there was no way to fix them. Smallpox had struck the Indians so there were no men to carry new wood from the forests. No treasure lay in the king's chest.

The Florida colony was subsidized by Nueva España. Since Florida protected the commerce between México and Spain, reasoned the crown, Nueva España must pay for the protection. Consequently, official in México City had to find the silver to pay the troops and buy the food, clothing and other supplies that Florida so desperately needed for existence. The royal decree to subsidize Florida was basic, of course. But collecting the money was quite another thing, as Floridians learned from bitter experience. The payments were always far behind and St. Augustine suffered poverty and extreme want.

Yet, if ever Florida needed a strong fort, it was now. The English had attacked Santo Domingo and captured Jamaica. The Dutch were known to be scouting Apalache Bay. As the corsairs grew bolder, one governor made this appraisal: "in spite of the great valor with which we would resist, successful defense would be doubtful" without stronger defenses.

Proposals for a permanent fort dated as early as 1586, soon after the discovery of the native shellstone called coquina. A few years later Governor Gonzalo Mendez de Canzo reported successful construction of a stone powder magazine and renewed enthusiasm for a masonry fort. The sandy, unstable coastal soil

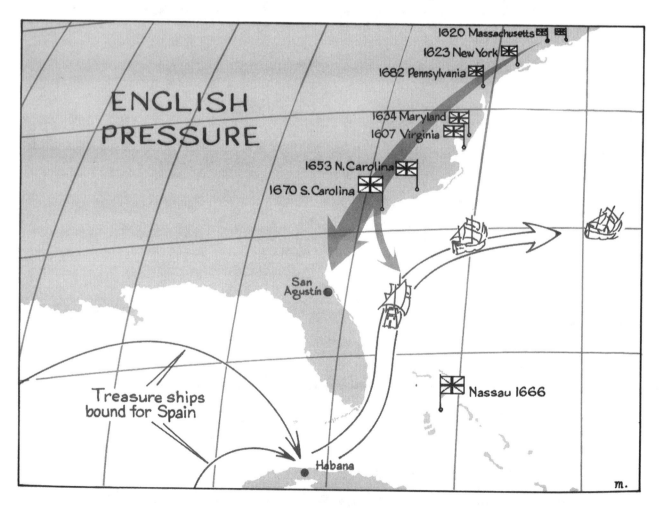

complicated the engineering problems, but the real obstacles were the poverty of the presidio and the feeling in Madrid that Florida did not really need strong defenses.

Even when the Spanish crown granted permission to build a stone fort (as happened more than once) circumstances proved that the time for the castillo had not yet come. Once a very practical governor, Diego de Rebolledo, cited the abundance of native materials, and outlined a step-by-step plan. All he wanted was prompt payment of the troop fund from Nueva España—a not unreasonable plea—and out of that money he would buy a dozen slaves versed in stonecutting and masonry, slaves such as were available in any number of Caribbean towns. To be sure the work was done right, he wanted the engineer from Cartagena assigned to the job. At the very least, he begged for the slaves: if nothing more, they could face the walls of the wooden fort with stone.

This well-considered project was tabled. A Florida representative, in Madrid seeking aid, unwittingly mentioned the old fort as being in "fair" condition, and the Council decided to wait for more information before doing anything.

With good reason, the Council seemed more concerned over other Florida problems. Food was even more important than forts, and the St. Augustine people were never far from starving times such as the spring of 1662, when provisions from Nueva España did not come. The frigate out of St. Augustine, bringing maize from the Indian granaries in western Florida, was also long overdue. The people feared she was lost. And this was the very time the treasurer chose to drop four old soldiers from the payroll. While the garrison was more or less inured to being ragged, underfed, and unpaid, the treasurer's decision utterly ruined morale. True, after 50 years in the crown's service, the ancient ones were not even good for guard duty. The treasurer was quite within his rights in dropping them. But his order was a death knell for the old veterans. The governor saw it as something worse—a damaging precedent. The younger soldiers would realize, argued the

governor, that "they were wasting the vigor of their youth and hoarding for themselves, as reward for their service, a death sentence by starvation in their old age."

The Council sided with the governor in this routine instance of bleak poverty, and no doubt the treasurer was glad to relieve his own conscience. Yet, even if officials in Spain recognized the shocking neglect, St. Augustine was still far from succor. The crown directed urgent new orders to the viceroy in México City: send the Florida payroll promptly every year. But matters did not improve. By 1668 more than 400,000 pesos—eight years' payments—were owing to Florida.

Then came the 1668 midnight raid. St. Augustine was utterly destitute. Once again the soldiers were faced with the prospect of digging roots by day and begging alms at night from the few more fortunate inhabitants of the presidio— or starvation. As for the old wooden fort, patchwork repairs had changed its design so that it violated every rule of defense. Because the beams under the gun platforms were rotten and so were the platforms, the cannon were useless. The sea had washed out the shoreline and waves crashed against the palisade.

Notwithstanding, the sack of St. Augustine was a blessing in disguise, for it shocked Spanish officialdom into action. The governor of Habana lent 1,200 pesos for masting and rigging the St. Augustine frigate, thus ensuring the presidio's communication with its supply bases. The viceroy released the 1669 payroll (76,172 pesos) plus 1,200 pesos for general repairs, weapons, gunpowder and lead for bullets. He also promised 75 men to bring the troops to authorized strength. Furthermore St. Augustine was allowed to keep an 18-pounder bronze cannon that had been salvaged from a shipwreck.

This aid—12 months of life for the colony— totaled at least 110,000 pesos. Included was the hire of mules for the 75 recruits to ride from México City to Veracruz. Hiring animals was easier than finding men, however, and getting the men aboard ship for the Florida frontier was harder yet. Fifty-one of them arrived at last in 1670 (the rest had deserted or died) but St. Augustine was not completely happy with their coming. They were mostly mulattoes, mestizos and men exiled by the criminal court. None was highly regarded by Major Ponce for courage in the royal cause.

It was Mariana, Queen Regent of Spain, who gave permanent aid to St. Augustine in three decrees addressed to the viceroy. On March 11, 1669, she ordered him to pay the Florida funds on time and add a proper amount for building the fortification proposed by the governor. Next, on April 10 she commanded him to support a full 300-man garrison in Florida (instead of the customary 257 soldiers and 43 missionaries). Finally, on October 30 she enjoined him to hear the views of the newly appointed Florida governor about an adequate fortification, and provide for its construction.

If the fear that pirates might return had finally convinced the crown that St. Augustine must have a strong fort in order to stay Spanish, and English settlement planted on Florida soil in April 1670 drove the point home. The English called it Charleston and said the land was Carolina. But the Floridians recognized the danger and saw the need to uproot the new colony before it waxed strong.

A trio of vessels sailed northward from St. Augustine. Then the winds blew stormy as they had for the French fleet before St. Augustine in 1565, the little Spanish fleet was scattered, and the fledgling English colony was saved. Mariana's treaty with England soon afterward

"Today, Sunday, about four in the afternoon, the second of October 1672...Manual de Cendoya, Governor and Captain General of these provinces for Her Majesty...with spade in hand...began the foundation trenches for construction of the Castillo..." Thus did the government notary attest the official ground breaking. Original in Archivo General de Indias.

recognized "established" settlements, so with the English only two days' sail away, St. Augustine could do nothing except prepare against invasion that was sure to come. The tiny garrison at Santa Catalina Mission (on St. Catherine's Island), in the coastal country south of Charleston, became the northern outpost. And construction of a citadel, built of imperishable stone, was soon to begin.

Beginning the Castillo

To succeed Governor Guerra, Mariana appointed Sergeant Major Don Manuel de Cendoya, a veteran of 22 years' service in Flanders, Italy, and Extremadura. Major Cendoya left Cadiz in July 1670 with his wife and their two infants.

In México City Cendoya followed Queen Mariana's orders and presented his views to the Viceroy, the Marquis de Mancera. Florida should be fortified at once with a main castillo at St. Augustine, a second fort to control the harbor mouth, and a third one to prevent troop landings. Thirty thousand pesos would be needed. Precisely at this point came the news of the Charleston settlement, and Cendoya at once suggested a fourth fort at Santa Catalina.

The viceroy's finance council finally decided to allot 12,000 pesos to begin work on one fort. If suitable progress were made, they would consider sending 10,000 yearly until completion. The question of additional forts would be referred to the crown. With this and a levy of 17 soldiers for the Florida service, Cendoya had to be satisfied. He left for Florida, making a stop at Habana where he sought skilled workmen—masons and lime burners. There he also found an engineer, Ignacio Daza.

It was on August 8, 1671, a month after Cendoya's arrival in St. Augustine, that the first workman began to draw his pay. By the time the mosquitoes were sluggish in the cooler fall weather, the quarrymen had opened the coquina pits on Anastasia Island, and the lime burners were building two big kilns just north of the old fort. The carpenters put up a palm-thatched shelter at the quarry; they built a dozen clumsy, square-end dugouts and laid decks over them for rafting the stone, the firewood and oyster shells for the limekilns; and they built boxes, handbarrows, and carretas—the long, narrow, hauling wagons. At his anvil, the blacksmith made a great noise, hammering out axes, picks, and stonecutters' hatchets, and putting on their steel edges; drawing iron into crowbars, or shovels, spades, hoes, and wedges; and for lighter work, making nails of all kinds and sizes for the carpenters. The grindstone screeched as the cutting edge went on the tools.

Indian peons at the quarry chopped out the dense thickets of scrub oak and palmetto, driving out the rattlesnakes and clearing the ground for the shovelmen to uncover the top layer of coquina. Day after day Diego Diaz Mejia, the overseer, kept the picks and axes going, cutting deep grooves into the soft yellow stone, while with wedge and bar the peons broke loose and pried up the rough blocks—small pieces that a single man could shoulder, and tremendously heavy, waterlogged cubes two feet thick and twice as long that six strong men could hardly lift from the bed of sandy shell. As a layer of stone was removed, again the shovelmen came in, taking off the newly exposed bed of loose shell and uncovering yet another and deeper stratum of rock. Down and down the quarrymen went until their pits reached water and they could go no farther.

Diaz watched his peons heave the finest stone on the wagons. He sent the oxen plodding to the wharf at the head of a marshy creek, where the load of rough stone was carefully balanced on the rafts for ferrying across the tide to the building site. And on the opposite shore of the bay, next to the old fort, the cache of unhewn stone daily grew larger, while the stonecutters piled their squares and chopped unceasingly to shape the soft coquina for the masons.

In the limekilns, oyster shells glowed white-hot and changed into fine quality, quick-setting lime. By spring of 1672, there were 4,000 fanegas (some 7,000 bushels) of lime in the two storehouses, and the great quantities of both hewn and rough stone were a welcome sight to people of St. Augustine.

Although the real construction was not even started, great obstacles had already been overcome. Very little masonry had ever been done in the presidio and, with the exception of the imported artisans, the workmen had to be trained. Even the imported ones had much to

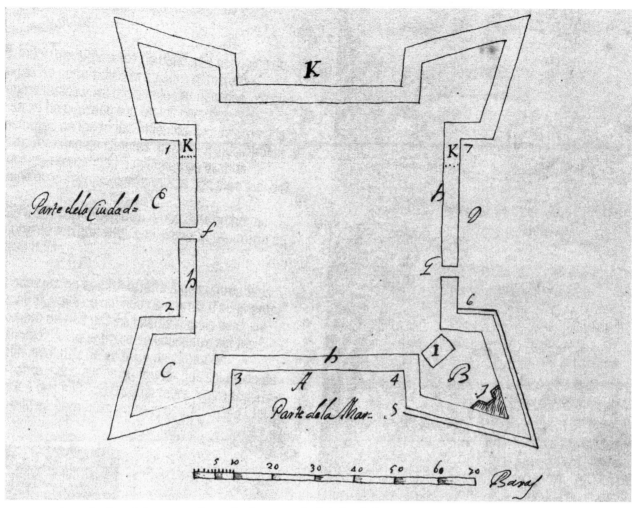

An early plan of the coquina fort in St. Augustine. Included with the report of Governor Salazar, May 1675.
Original manuscript in Archives of the Indies, Seville, Spain.

learn about coquina, the natural shellstone peculiar to this part of Florida. Coquina consists of broken sea shells cemented together by their own lime. Where a shelly stratum was under great geological pressure, the stone is solid and relatively hard; where conditions were less favorable, it is coarse and easily crumbled. The men had to become expert in grading the stone, for only the best of it could go into the walls.

There was also a shortage of common labor. When there should have been 150 men to keep the 15 artisans working at top speed—50 in the quarries and hauling stone, 50 for gathering oyster shells and helping at the kilns, and another 50 for digging the foundation trenches, toting the excavation baskets, and mixing mortar—it was hard to get as many as 100 laborers on the job.

Indians from three nations, the Guale

(coastal Georgia), Timucua (Florida east of the Aucilla River) and Apalache (between the Aucilla and the Apalachicola), were tapped for manpower. True, they were paid labor, but some had to travel 80 leagues to reach the presidio, and many served unwillingly. The Spanish levies for labor caused serious domestic problems, for the draftees had either to bring their families along or else leave them in the home villages to eke out their own living. In theory each complement of Indian labor served only a certain length of time; in practice it was not uncommon for the men to be held long past their assigned time, either through necessity or carelessness. In some cases, not even the chiefs were exempt from the draft.

The Indian was cheap labor—one real (about $0.20) per day, plus rations of maize. But good labor he was not. A brave might play the

Coquina Quarry, Anastasia Island.

bone-breaking game of Indian ball for hours on end, but the day-in, day-out, back-straining labor of the quarries was more than he could take. Some of the Indians, however, developed into carpenters, and though they did not get the top way of 10 to 12 reales, they seemed well pleased with their 8 reales—which was twice the pay of an apprentice carpenter. Another Indian, Andres, learned the stonecutter's craft and worked on the Castillo for 16 years.

In addition to Indian labor, there were a few Spanish peons (paid 4 reales per day) and a number of convicts, either local or from Caribbean ports. Beginning with 1679 there were seven Negroes and mulattoes among the convicts. Eighteen black slaves belonging to the crown joined the labor gang in 1687. Convicts and slaves received rations but no wage. A

typical convict might have been the Spaniard caught smuggling English goods into the colony. He was condemned to six years' labor on the fortifications. If he tried to escape, the term was doubled and he faced the grim prospect of being sent to a fever-infested African presidio to work it out.

The military engineer, Ignacio Daza, was paid the top wage of 3 pesos (about $4.75) per day. Daza died seven months after coming to Florida, so the crown paid only the surprisingly small sum of 546 pesos (about $862) for engineering services in starting the greatest of Spanish Florida fortifications.

Of the artisans, there were Lorenzo Lajones, master of construction, and a pair of master masons, each of whom received the master workman's wage of 20 reales (about $4). In

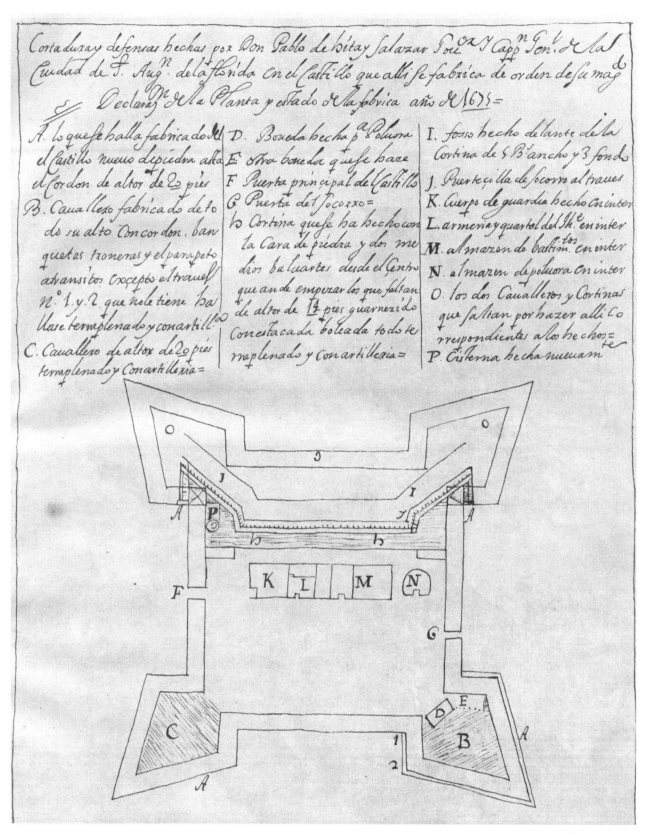

The sketch shows the progress of construction by July 9, 1675. Only the north, south and east walls walls were up. To make the fort defensible, Governor Hita Salazar closed the west side with an earthwork (h) until the permanent walls could be built. Temporary buildings were for guardroom (k), armory and lieutenant's quarters (L), provisions (M) and gunpowder (N). There was also a vaulted magazine (D) for powder; another vault (E) begun but never finished; the main gate (F); a postern (G), later sealed; and a well (P). Original manuscript in Archives of the Indies, Seville, Spain.

addition there were seven masons and eight stonecutters at 12 reales, and a dozen carpenters whose pay ranged from 6 to 12 reales. Later, some of these wages were reduced: Lajones' successor as master of construction was paid only 17 reales, the master mason 13, and the stonecutters from 3 to 11 reales, with half of them at the 3-and 4-real level.

These were few men for the job at hand, and to speed the work along Governor Cendoya used prisoners from the Carolina colony. Ironically enough, their worth far exceeded their numbers in building this defense against their countrymen. Back in 1670, a vessel bound for Charleston mistakenly put in at Santa Catalina Mission, the Spanish post near the Savannah River. William Carr and John Rivers were captured. A rescue sloop came boiling out of Charleston and Joseph Bailey and John took a blustering message ashore to the Spaniards. For their pains, they were dispatched with Rivers and Carr to St. Augustine where, from time to time, they were reluctantly joined by others of their countrymen.

The governor did not hesitate long in putting them to work. Three of the prisoners were masons, and their Spanish names—Bernardo Patricio (for Bernard Fitzpatrick), and Juan Calens (for John Collins), and Guillermo Car (for William Carr)—were duly written on the payrolls. Some of these British subjects became permanent residents. Carr, for instance, embraced first the Catholic faith and then Juana de Contreras, by whom he fathered eight children. His father-in-law was a corporal, a circumstance which may have helped Carr to enlist as a gunner while also working as a highly paid stonecutter.

The Spanish were understandably cautious in relying on the loyalty of foreigners, but actually the new subjects served well. John Collins especially pleased the officials. He could burn more lime in a week than others could in twice the time. Also to the point, as a prisoner he had to be paid only 8 reales instead of the 20 due a master workman. Like Carr, Collins seemed to like St. Augustine. He rose steadily in

the crown's employ from master of the kilns to quarrymaster, with dugouts, provisions, and convicts all in his charge. When pirates landed on Anastasia in 1683 and marched on the city, instead of joining them he made sure that all crown property in the quarry was moved to safety. Royal recognition of his zeal and loyalty honored his 19 years or more of service.

Another unusual case occurred a few years later. Some leagues north of St. Augustine, 11 Englishmen were captured. All were committed to the labor gang—except Andrew Ransom. He was to be garroted. On the appointed day Ransom ascended the scaffold. The executioner put the rope collar about his neck. The screw was turned 6 times—and the rope broke! Ransom breathed again.

While the onlookers marveled, the friars took the incident as an act of God and led Ransom to sanctuary in the parish church. Word reached the governor that this man was an ingenious fellow, an artillerist, a carpenter, and what was most remarkable, a maker of "artificial fires." Ransom was offered "protection" if he would put his talents to use at the castillo. He agreed and, like Collins, was exceedingly helpful, for no one else had such abilities. Twelve long years later, church authorities finally agreed that the sanctuary granted by the parish pastor was valid. At last Ransom was free of the garrote.

All told, there were close to 150 men on the construction crew in those first days of feverish preparations. They, along with some 500 others, including about 100 effective soldiers in the garrison, a few Franciscan friars, a dozen mariners, and the townspeople, had to be fed. When supplies from Nueva España did not come, getting food was even harder than finding workmen, especially since the coastal soil at St. Augustine yielded poorly to seventeenth century agriculture.

Indian corn (maize) was the staple. Most of the planting, cultivating, and harvesting of extensive fields near the town was done by Indians brought from their provinces to do the work. At times as many as 300 Indians served the crown in the presidio, counting those at work on the fortification. They were furnished rations of maize—3 pounds daily until 1679, then 2-1/2 pounds until 1687, and finally 2-1/2 again—during their time in St. Augustine or on the journey home over the wilderness trails. Convicts also got maize rations if flour was not on hand.

Maize cost the crown 7 reales per arroba (25 pounds) and an arroba lasted the average Indian only 10 days. Flour form Spain cost 10 reales per arroba; the master workmen, the English masons, and the Spanish convicts got rations form this store. The convicts also received a meat ration. Fresh meat was rather scarce, but the waters teemed with fish and there were plenty of shellfish. A paid fisherman kept the men supplied.

Garden vegetables were few. Squash grew well in the sandy soil, and beans and sweet potatoes, citron, pomegranates, figs. Oranges thrived. And of course there were onions and garlic. But it must be remembered that St.

Augustine was never self-supporting. After a century of existence, it still depended for its very life upon the subsidy from Nueva España. As the long, hot days of the second summer shortened into fall, Governor Cendoya saw that after a year of gathering men and materials, he was ready to start building.

No long-drawn-out survey and detailed study helped to locate the new fort, for the Spanish had learned their lessons by a century and more of experiment on the shores of Matanzas Bay. Engineer Daza and Governor Cendoya, meeting with a general council, decided the castillo should be on the west shore of the bay just north of the old fort. It was a site that took advantage of every natural defense feature. Here the enemy would find it almost impossible to bring heavy siege guns within range. A shallow bar at the harbor entrance kept out the bigger warships. All vessels coming in had to pass under the fort guns.

Both town and fort were on a narrow

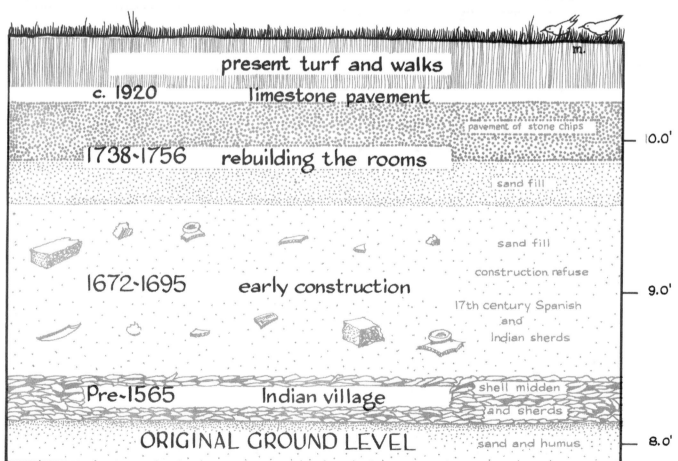

Archeology in the Castillo Courtyard shows the calendar of human occupancy from prehistory to now.

When supplies from Nueva España did not come, getting food was even harder than finding workmen, especially since the coastal soil at St. Augustine yielded poorly to seventeenth century agriculture. Indian corn (maize) was the staple. Most of the planting, cultivating, and harvesting of extensive fields near the town was done by Indians brought from their provinces to do the work.

peninsula with water or impassable marsh on three sides. The fourth side—the northern neck where the fort stood—was constricted by a meandering creek. Beyond the marshes was wilderness—the pine barrens and cypress swamps, oak groves and palmetto scrubs. Roads were mere Indian trails, and the quickest passage from one coastal outpost to the next was by dugout along the inland waterway. Attackers might march down the coast on the wide, hard beaches (provided they could get across the estuaries on the way), but they still had to pass over broad bay and salt marsh before they could reach the fort.

Daza and the governor liked the plan of the old fort. The new one, they decided, would be similar, though somewhat larger to make more

room for quarters, guardroom, chapel, wells, ovens, powder magazine, and other essential rooms. In line with the more recent ideas, Daza recommended a slight lengthening of the bastions. All around the castillo they planned a broad, deep moat and beyond it, a high palisade on the three land sides.

It was a simple and unpretentious plan, but a good one. Daza, schooled in the Italian-Spanish principles of fortification grown out of the sixteenth century designs of Franceso de Marchi, was clearly a practical man. His plan called for a "regular" fort—that is, a symmetrical structure. Basically it was simply a square with a bastion at each corner. Equally strong on all sides, this design was ideal for Florida's low, flat terrain.

The Years of Construction

About four o'clock Sunday afternoon, October 2, 1672, Governor Cendoya walked to a likely looking spot between the strings marking out the lines of the new fortification. He thrust a spade into the earth, and thus broke ground for Castillo de San Marcos, worthy successor to the name that for almost 100 years had been used for the forts of St. Augustine presidio.

The official witnesses were present, including the notary, Juan Moreno y Segovia, who recorded the event for the information of Queen Mariana. Moreno faithfully certified that not only was the work started on this Sunday afternoon, but it continued; and at most of it he, the notary, was present. (He also mentioned that he had to use ordinary paper because St. Augustine had no official stamped paper.)

Little more than a month later on Wednesday, November 9, Cendoya laid the first stone of the foundation. The people of St. Augustine must have wept for joy. All were glad and proud, the aged soldiers who had given a lifetime of service to the crown, the four little orphans whose father died in the pirate raid a few years earlier, the widows and their children, the craftsmen, the workmen, the royal officials (some of whom now served as their fathers had before them); but none could have been more pleased or proud than Don Manuel de Cendoya. He of all the Florida governors had the honor to begin the first permanent Florida fortification of Her Catholic Majesty.

Laying the foundations was not easy, for the soil was sandy and low and as winter came the Indian peons were struck by El Contagio—The Contagion. The laboring force dwindled to nothing. The governor asked the crown to have Habana send 30 Negro slaves. Meanwhile, Cendoya himself and his soldiers took to the shovels. As they dug a trench some 17 feet wide and 5 feet deep, the masons came in and laid two courses of heavy stones directly on the hard-packed sand bottom. Slow work it was, for high tide flooded the trenches.

About 1-1/2 feet inside the toe of this broad 2-foot-high foundation, the masons stretched a line marking the scarp or curtain, a wall that would gradually taper upward form a 13-foot base to about 9 feet at its top, 20 feet above the foundation. In the 12 months that followed, the north, south, and east walls rose steadily. By midsummer of 1673 the east side was 12 feet high and the presidio was jubilant over the news that Nueva España was sending 10,000 pesos for carrying on.

This good news was tempered by the viceroy's assertion that he would release no more money for the work without a direct order from the crown. Cendoya had already asked Her Majesty to raise the allowance to 16,000 pesos a year so the construction could be finished in four years. For, as he put it, the English menace at Charleston brooked no delay. The English were said to be outfitting ships for an invasion.

But slowly and more slowly the building went. In 1673 Cendoya and Daza died within a few days of one another. The governor's mantle fell upon Major Ponce, in whom the local Spaniards had little confidence.

Trouble beset poor Ponce on every side. The viceroy was discouragingly reluctant to part with money for this project, despite evidence that English strength was increasing daily, especially among the Indians. A terrific storm hit St. Augustine. High tides undermined houses, flooded fields and gardens, and polluted the wells. Sickness took its toll of peon and townsman alike.

The storm totally ruined the old wooden fort. Waves washed out a bastion, causing it to collapse under the weight of its guns. The other seaward bastion and the palisade were also breached in several places.

Then in the spring of 1675 another provision ship was lost. Ponce had to take the peons on a long march into Timucua to fetch provisions from the Indians. Only the handful of masons were left to carry on the work at the Castillo.

Working on the east wall, 1675

Despite all his troubles, Ponce made considerable progress during his acting governorship. The north curtain was the full 20 feet high and ready for its cordon. The east curtain was up 15 feet and the south curtain 12. The seaward bastions were also well along. In the courtyard Ponce had started some temporary but essential facilities—guardroom, powder magazine, and storerooms—with lumber salvaged form the old fort. But looking west from the courtyard the soldiers could see only open country; there was no west wall as yet.

On May 3, 1675, the long-awaited ship from Nueva España safely crossed the bar with supplies and a new governor for Florida. Sergeant Major Don Pablo de Hita Salazar was a hard-bitten veteran of campaigns in Flanders, Germany and Badajoz, and most recently governor of Veracruz. His career in the royal service had been "no other than the arquebus and the pike," and surely it was as a soldier of reputation that he was assigned to Florida, for in addition to carrying on the fortification work he was charged to "dislocate" the Charleston settlement. Led to believe the viceroy would help in the difficult task ahead, Hita in fact found that official singularly reluctant. Before releasing any monies at all, the viceroy insisted that Hita make a report on Castillo construction as soon as he got to Florida. At last the old fellow left the viceregal presence in disgust.

At St. Augustine, while it was clear the work had been dragging, he found things that pleased him: "Although I have seen many castillos of consequence and reputation," he wrote the crown, "in the form of its plan this one is not surpassed by any of those of greater character." Furthermore, he endorsed the statement of the royal officials, who were eager to point out the brighter side of the picture: "if it had to be built in another place than St. Augustine it would cost a double amount because there will not be the advantage of having the peons, at a real of wages each day, with such meagre sustenance as three pounds of maize, nor will the overseers and artisans work in other places with such little salaries…Nor will the stone, lime, and other material be found so close at hand and with the convenience there is in this presidio."

Perhaps these citations of economies were apologetic, because 34,298 pesos had already been spent on the new fort, and still it was no more protection than a pile of stone. Nor was the old fort any defense. If a gunner dared to touch his match to a cannon, the concussion might flatten the rest of the old ruin. The enemy at Charleston was less than 70 leagues away; his 200 fighting men outnumbered the Spanish effectives, while English deserters reported that Charleston was well defended by a stockade fort with about 20 cannon.

Using characteristic realism, and energy and enthusiasm that would have done credit to a much younger man, Don Pablo set about making his own fortification defensible. The bastion of San Carlos—the northeast salient of the Castillo—was the nearest to completion. Hita ordered it finished so that cannon could be mounted on its rampart.

While the masons were busy at that work, he took his soldiers and razed the old fort. The best of its wood went into a barrier across the open west end of the Castillo. In 15 days they built a 12-foot-high earthwork with two half-bastions, faced with a veneer of stone and fronted by a moat 14 feet wide and 10 feet deep. At last the garrison had four walls for protection.

Next the powder magazine in the gorge of San Carlos was completed and a ramp laid over it to give access to the rampart above. The three curtains rose to their full height of 20 feet. At the southeast corner the peons dumped hundreds of baskets of sand and rubble into the void formed by the walls of San Agustin bastion, and filled it to the 20-foot level.

Both carpenters and masons worked on the temporary buildings. A convenient little powder magazine was finished near the north curtain. A long, narrow, wooden structure, partitioned into guardhouse, lieutenant's quarters, armory and provision magazine, took shape along the west wall. Finally, a few of the guns from the old fort were mounted in San Carlos and San Agustin

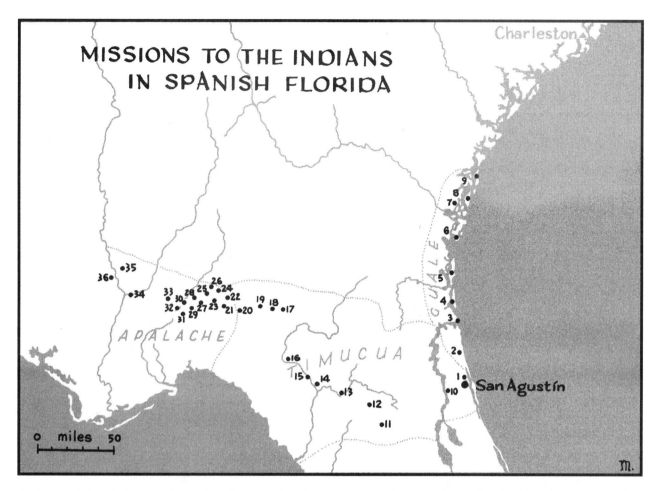

MISSIONS TO THE INDIANS IN SPANISH FLORIDA

Spain regarded the Indians as wards of the Crown, to be Christianized and Hispanicized into allies. By 1680 the Franciscans had built missions in many popluation centers. The Timucua, Apalache and Guale nations supplied much of the food (maize) and labor for building the Castillo. But between 1680 and 1706 heathen Indian raids, often English-led, enslaved or absorbed most of these Spanish allies, leaving St. Augustine vulnerable to attack.

Numbers on the map show approximate locations of known missions: 1-Nombre de Dios. 2-La Natividad de Nuestra Senora de Tolomato. 3-San Juan del Puerto. 4-Santa Maria. 5-San Felipe. 6-Santa Buenaventura. 7-Santo Domingo de Asaho. 8-San Jose de Zapala. 9-Santa Catalina. 10-San Diego Salamototo. 11-San Francisco de Potano. 12- Santa Fe de Tolaca. 13-Santa Catalina de Afuica.14-Santa Cruz de Ajohica. 15-Santa Cruz de Tarihica. 16-San Juan de Guacara. 17-Santa Elena de Machaba. 18-San Pedro de Potohiriba. 19-San Mateo. 20-San Miguel de Asyle. 21-La Concepcion de Ayubali. 22-San Lorenzo de Hibatachuco. 23-San Juan de Aspalaga. 24-San Francisco de Aconi. 25-San Pedro de Patali. 26-San Jose de Acuya. 27-San Antonio de Bacuqua. 28-San Damian de Cupahica. 29-San Luis de Talimali. 30-La Purificacion de Tama.31-San Martin de Capoli. 32-Santa Cruz de Capoli. 33-La Asuncion del Puerto. 34-Santa Cruz de Sabacola. 35-San Carlos. 36-San Nicolas.

bastions and along the west front. After three years of work, the Castillo was a defense at last.

And now Governor Hita's first admiration for its design vanished. The Castillo, he said, was too massive. Surely no one would ever besiege it formally. Rather, the danger lay in a blockade of the harbor or occupation of Anastasia Island, actions that would cut the presidio lifeline. San Carlos bastion was too high for effective fire on the inlet or to sweep

Anastasia. He argued that the Castillo should be held to a total height of only 20 feet (including the parapet), and supplemented by a 6-gun redoubt directly facing the inlet.

The royal officials strenuously opposed the governor's attempts to change Daza's plan. Naturally they wrote the crown of Hita's desire to tear finished walls down to the level he thought proper.

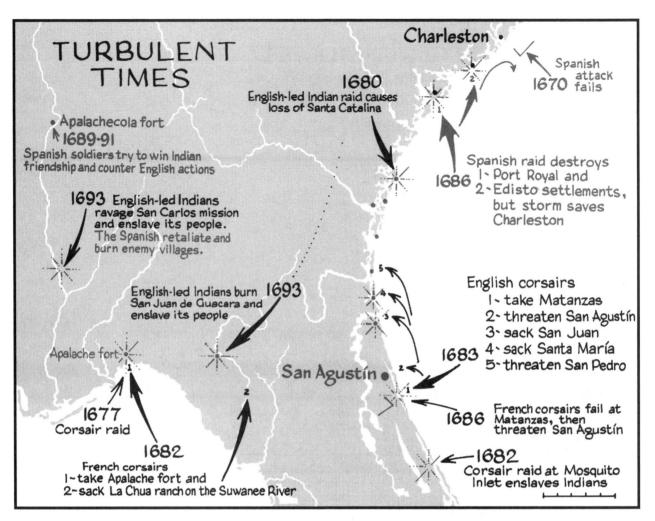

TURBULENT TIMES

Charleston •

Spanish attack fails
1670

1680
English-led Indian raid causes loss of Santa Catalina

• Apalachecola fort
↑ **1689-91**
Spanish soldiers try to win Indian friendship and counter English actions

1693 English-led Indians ravage San Carlos mission and enslave its people. The Spanish retaliate and burn enemy villages.

Spanish raid destroys
1686 1 - Port Royal and
2 - Edisto settlements, but storm saves Charleston

English-led Indians burn San Juan de Guacara and enslave its people **1693**

English corsairs
1 - take Matanzas
2 - threaten San Agustín
3 - sack San Juan
4 - sack Santa María
5 - threaten San Pedro
1683

San Agustín •

Apalache fort •
1

1677
Corsair raid

French corsairs fail at Matanzas, then threaten San Agustín
1686

1682
French corsairs
1 - take Apalache fort and
2 - sack La Chua ranch on the Suwanee River

←**1682**
Corsair raid at Mosquito Inlet enslaves Indians

In Hita's view the west wall, though temporary, was adequate. Therefore he would defer the permanent wall and start instead on the permanent guardroom, quarters, ravelin and moat. Not so, his advisors pointed out. The west wall was nothing but half-rotten poles and a mound of earth faced with stone. The important thing was to complete all the walls as soon as possible.

In the hope that the crown would agree to lower the walls, Hita let the finished work lag on the two seaward bastions while he began the west wall and bastions. Construction continued in spite of trouble with the Choctaws, in spite of the worrisome impossibility of driving out the Carolina settlers, in spite of the pirate raid on the port of Apalache in the west and the ever-present fear of invasion. Lorenzo Lajones died (he was master of construction); still the work went on. Even after the viceroy's 10,000 pesos were spent, the job was kept going with money diverted from the troop payroll. As a last resort,

people gave what they could out of their own poverty. When these gifts were gone, the scrape of the trowel ceased and the hammer and axe were laid aside. Castillo construction stopped on the last day 1677.

The supply vessel bringing desperately needed provisions and clothing sailed safely all the way from Nueva España, only to be lost on a sand bar right in St. Augustine harbor. It was a heartbreaking loss. Hita became disconsolate. The help he begged from Habana never came; and for four years his reports to the viceroy had been ignored. Old, discouraged, sick, Hita wrote the crown that he was "without human recourse" in this remote province. Perhaps the final blow to his pride was a terse order from the crown to stick strictly to Daza's plan for the Castillo.

Yet the old warrior did not give up. Eventually the viceroy released 5,000 more pesos and after 20 months of idleness construction resumed on August 29, 1679. As soon as Hita got up from his sickbed he was back at the fort, impatient with the snail's pace of progress under a new master of construction. The new man was Juan Marquez Molina of Habana, whose sharp-eyed inspections found stones missing from their courses and some of the walls too thin.

The royal officials, always on hand to make sure the governor followed the crown's directives to the letter, blamed these deficiencies on Hita, "who had trod this fort down without knowledge of the art of fortification." With another 5,000 pesos plus the masons due to arrive from Habana, said the old man in rebuttal, "I promise to leave the work in very good condition." Before he could make good on that promise, Sergeant Major Don Juan Marquez Cabrera arrived at the end of November 1680 to take over the reins of government.

So, half apologizing for his own little knowledge of "architecture and geometry," Hita left the trials and tribulations of this frontier province to his more youthful successor.

Actually, Hita had done a great deal. Within six weeks after his arrival he had made the Castillo defensible against any but an overwhelming force. During the rest of his 5 1/2-year term, over one obstacle after another, he had brought the walls up to where they were ready for the parapet builders. In fact, the parapet on San Carlos bastion was almost complete, with embrasures for the artillery and firing steps for the musketeers. The only low part of the work was the San Pablo bastion, where the level had been miscalculated. The sally port had its drawbridge and iron-bound portal, and another heavy door closed the postern in the east curtain. Permanent rooms that would go along the curtain walls were still only plans, but in a temporary building centered in the courtyard were a guardroom and storeroom, and a little chapel stood near the postern in the shadow of the east curtain.

The new man, Major Juan Marquez Cabrera, formerly governor of Honduras, checked the Castillo work carefully with the construction master. Those long years without an engineer had left them a heritage of mistakes—skimpy foundations, levels miscalculated—which had to be set right. From Habana came a military engineer, Ensign Don Juan de Ciscara. During his brief stay he gave valuable guidance for continuing the work, built the ramp to San Pablo bastion, and laid foundations for the ravelin and its moat wall.

The 1680's were turbulent years. In 1682, the year the ravelin was finished, a dozen or so pirate craft in the Bahama Channel seized numerous Spanish prizes, including the Florida frigate on its way to Veracruz. They raided Mosquito Inlet, only 60 miles south of St. Augustine. In the west, pirates struck Fort San Marcos de Apalache and even went up the San Martin (Suwanee) River to rob cattle ranches in Timucua.

Nor did the Castillo building go smoothly. Apprehensive of invasion and hoping to speed up construction, Governor Marquez asked the curate for permission to work his men on holy days. There was ample precedent for this concession, but Marquez had never got on well with the religious, and they refused. As a result, the peons could not bring in materials. Construction fell far behind schedule. Marquez appealed the decision to higher church authorities. Eventually they gave permission to work Sundays and holidays, but only during emergencies, and then solely on the fort itself. The dispensation such as it was, arrived too late; the expected invasion came first.

On March 30, 1683, English corsairs landed a few leagues south of the Centinela de Matanzas, the watchtower at Matanzas Inlet near the south end of Anastasia Island and about 14 miles from St. Augustine. Under cover of darkness, a few of the raiders came up behind the tower and surprised the sentries, who were either asleep or not on the alert.

The march on St. Augustine began the next day. Fortunately a soldier from St. Augustine happened by Matanzas and saw the motley band. Posthaste he warned the governor, who sent Captain Antonio de Arguelles with 30 musketeers to meet them on Anastasia.

A mile from the presidio the pirates walked into the captain's ambush—straight into a withering fire. After a few exchange shots—one of which lodged in Arguelles' leg—they beat a hasty retreat back down the island to their boats. Then they sailed to St. Augustine and anchored at the inlet in plain sight of the unfinished Castillo.

Marquez, his soldiers, the men, and even the women of the town were working day and night to strengthen the Castillo. Missing parapets and firing steps were improvised from dry stone. Expecting the worst, everybody crowded into the fort. But the corsairs, looking at the stone fort and nursing their wounds, decided to sail on.

After the excitement, the Castillo crew worked with renewed zeal. By mid-1683 they had completed the San Agustin and San Pablo bastions. Governor Marquez sent the crown a wooden model to show what had been done.

This was progress made in the face of privation—hunger that made the people demand of Marquez that he buy supplies from a stray Dutch trader from New York. It was unlawful, but the people had to eat. Imagine the joy in the presidio soon afterward when two subsidy payments came at one time! Marquez gave the soldiers two years' back pay and had enough provisions on hand for 14 months. The 27 guns of the presidio from the little iron 2-pounder to the heavy 40-pounder bronze, all had their gunner's ladle, rammer, sponge, and wormer, along with plenty of powder and shot. And now there was also an alarm bell in San Carlos bastion.

By August 1684 Governor Marquez was ready to start on the fort rooms, and they were finished in the spring of 1685. Courtyard walls paralleled the four curtains, and foot-square beams spanned the distance between them. Laid over these great beams were 3-inch planks, which supported a slab roof of tabby masonry. On the north were the powder magazine and two big storerooms. Quarters were along the west curtain, guardroom and chapel on the south, and rooms on the east included a latrine and prison. Altogether there were more than 20 rooms.

The only major work yet to do was beyond the walls. The surrounding moat, 40 feet wide, needed a couple of feet in depth. Only part of the moat wall was up to its full 8-foot height. In fact, of the outworks only the ravelin was finished.

But with the fortification thus far along, Governor Marquez could give more attention to other business, such as Lord Cardross' Scottish colony at Port Royal (S.C.). This was, in the Spanish view, a new and obnoxious settlement that encouraged heathen Indians to raid the mission

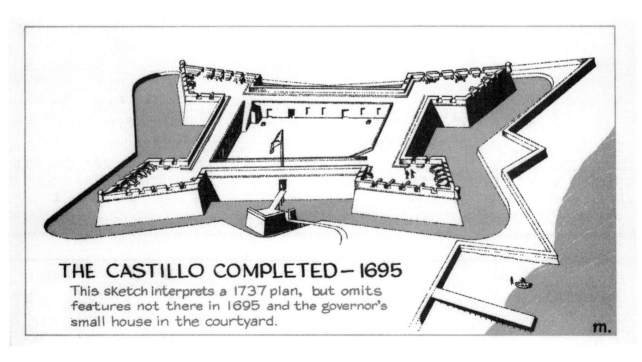

THE CASTILLO COMPLETED — 1695
This sketch interprets a 1737 plan, but omits features not there in 1695 and the governor's small house in the courtyard.

m.

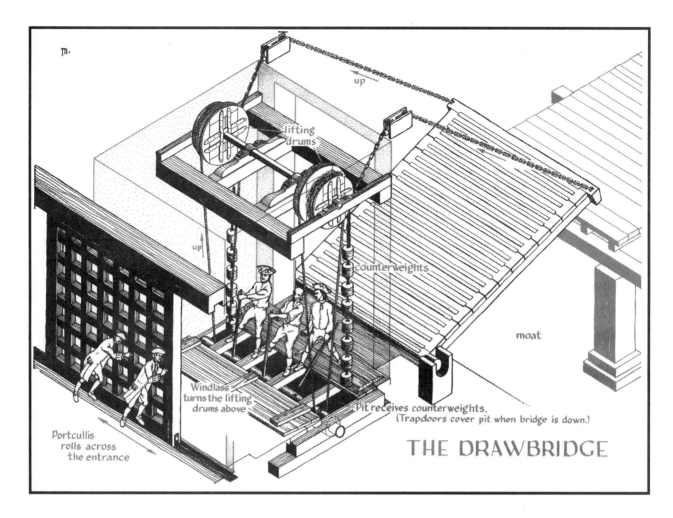

m.

up

lifting
drums

up

counterweights

moat

Windlass
turns the lifting
drums above.

Pit receives counterweights.
(Trapdoors cover pit when bridge is down.)

Portcullis
rolls across
the entrance

THE DRAWBRIDGE

Indians. Furthermore, it was in land recognized as Spanish even by the English monarch.

So out from St. Augustine in the stormy month of September 1686, Marquez sent Captain Alejandro Tomas de Leon, a corsair form Habana, with three galliots. Leon destroyed the Cardross colony and then sacked and burned Governor Morton's plantation on Edisto Island.

Next the Spaniards set a course for Charleston but again, as had happened in 1670, a storm blew them away from the hated English colony. Leon's vessel, the Rosario, was lost and he along with it. Another of the trio was beached, and the last of the little armada limped slowly back to St. Augustine.

Actually the real contest for the southeast had already begun, and the action was in the hinterlands far from the coast. English traders led the advance from Charleston; and to bolster the Indians against them, Governor Marquez sent soldiers and missionaries from St. Augustine to the Apalachecola nation in western Georgia.

For the Spanish, it was a losing fight—an exciting, exasperating struggle of diplomacy and intrigue, trade and cupidity, war and religion, slavery and death. Marquez personally was also losing another battle—his bid to reduce the power of the clergy in Florida affairs. The end came in April 1687 when the padres denied him confession. Marquez left his post and fled to Habana.

Captain of cuirassiers Diego de Quiraoga y Losada took possession of the office on August 21, 1687. That same day he stopped work on the Castillo because there was no way to feed the workmen. These troubles and the certainty of reprisals from the Carolinians sent Captain Juan de Ayala Escobar directly to Spain for help. He came back with 80 soldiers, the money for maintaining them, and even a Negro slave to help in the fields. The black man, one of a dozen Ayala had hoped to deliver, was a much-needed addition to the colony, and Captain Ayala was welcomed back to St. Augustine with rejoicing "for his good diligence."

Soon there was more black labor for both fields and fortifications. From the Carolina plantations, an occasional slave would slip away, searching his way southward along the waterways. In 1687 a small boat loaded with eight runaways and a baby girl made its way to St. Augustine. The men found work to do and the governor took the two women into his household for servants. It was a fairly happy arrangement: the slaves worked well and soon asked for Catholic baptism.

A few months later, William Dunlop came from Charleston in search of them. Governor Quiroga, reluctant to surrender converted slaves, offered to buy them for the Spanish crown. Dunlop agreed to the sale, even though the governor was as usual short of cash and had to pay by promise. To seal the bargain, Dunlop gave the baby her freedom. Later the crown liberated the others.

Since in the first place commerce with Carolina was illegal, and in the second place the crown could not buy freedom for every stray that came to Florida, that year of 1687 had introduced a knotty problem. More and more Carolina blacks left their English master. Few could ever be reclaimed. Growing more serious with each year, the slave trouble cancelled any hope of amicable relations between the Spanish and English colonists. Eventually the Spanish decreed freedom for all Carolina slaves coming to Florida, and the governor established a fortified village for them hardly more than a cannon shot from the Castillo.

Construction work resumed in the spring of 1688, after a shipment of corn came from Apalache. In Habana for 137 pesos Governor Quiroga bought a stone bearing the royal arms to be set into the wall over the gate. At this time, too the little town entered its "stone age," for as surplus materials from the crown quarries became available, masonry buildings gradually took the place of the board-and-thatch housing that had been traditional here since the founding.

Until the outworks could be finished, the Castillo was vulnerable to siege guns and scaling ladders. Nevertheless it was impossible to push

the heavy work of quarrying, lumbering, and hauling at this crucial time. There were too many other pressures. Belatedly trying to counteract English gains and strengthen their own ties with the Indians, the Spanish built a field fort in the Apalachecola country. Unfortunately the soldiers had to be pulled back to St. Augustine as Spain declared war on France in 1689.

This time Spain and England were on the same side of the fence against France. Yet Governor Quiroga wondered at the presence of English vessels off both northern and southern coasts. He also wrote a false letter telling of a strength far beyond what he had, against the chance that enemies might capture the packet carrying the true news of St. Augustine's weakness. For again the supply situation was critical, and swarms of French corsairs infested the waters between Florida and Habana. Two provision vessels were lost on the Keys and a third fell into French hands. Until food eventually came in from Habana and Campeche, the soldiers had to live on handouts from the townspeople.

To lessen the chances of famine in the future, the Florida officials resolved to plant great fields of maize nearby. And where was better than the broad, fallow clearings around the fort? Acres of waving corn soon covered the land almost up to the moat. When the crown heard of these plantings, back to Florida came a royal order banning maize fields within a musket shot of the Castillo. A whole army could hide in the tall corn without being seen by the sentries!

A new governor, Don Laureano de Torres y Ayala, arrived in 1693. At the outset he had to deal with hostilities between St. Augustine and Charleston—hostilities which mocked the Spanish-English alliance in Europe. Already the Indian village of San Juan de Guacara (on the Suwanee River) had been burned and some of its people abducted by English-led Uchees and Yamassees. Now, encouraged by the English, Apalachecola Indians raided San Carlos in Apalache, robbing the church and carrying 42 Christian Indians away into slavery. A Spanish

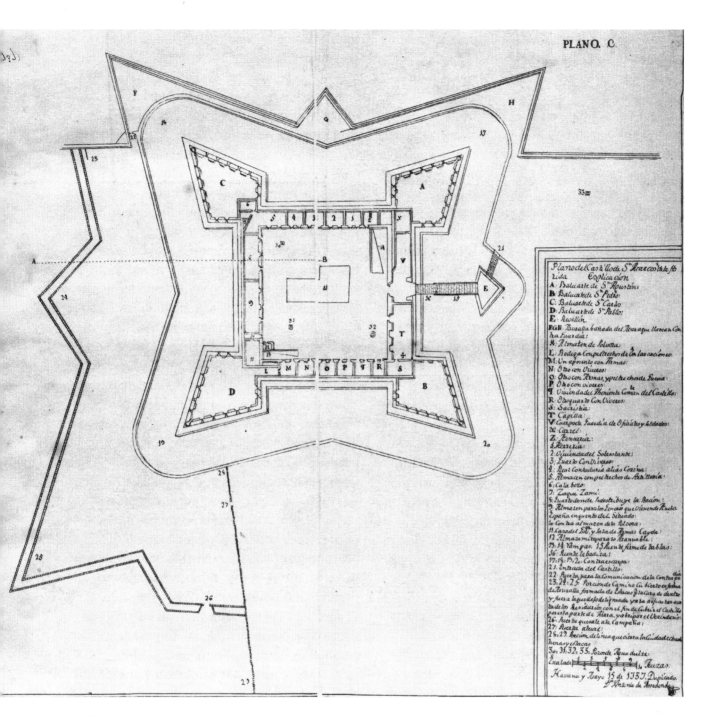

A 1737 plan by Royal Engineer Antonio de Arredondo shows the Castillo just before the major changes made in the middle 1700's. The key reads: A-Bastion of San Agustin. B-Bastion of San Pedro. C-Bastion of San Carlos. D-Bastion of San Pablo. E-Ravelin. FGH-Wall washed by the sea, called the counterguard. K-Powder magazine. L-Storeroom with ship's stores. M-Room with arms. N-Room with provisions. O-Room with arms and military stores. P-Room with provisions. Q-Quarters of the lieutenant governor of the Castillo. R-Room with provisions. S-Sacristy. T-Chapel. V-Guardroom for officers and men. X-Jail. Z.The necessary. 1-Smithy. 2-Quarters of the overseer. 3-Room with provisions. 4-Accountancy alias kitchen. 5-Storeroom with artillery stores. 6-Calaboose. 7-Small closet. 8-Room where the rations are distributed. 9-Storeroom for the situado (subsidy) goods from New Spain. 10-Powder magazine entrance. 11-Governor's Quarters and arms room, in ruins. 12-Storeroom for small stores. 13-14-Ramps. 15-Fixed bridge of planks. 16-Drawbridge. 17-18-19-20-Counterscarp. 21-Entrance to the Castillo. 22-Gate for communication with the counterguard. 23-24-25-Part of the covered way, in the shape of a wall with stakes on the inner and outer faces, which was traced out. It is to be built by convicts, with the objective of covering the Castillo on this land side and to shelter the townspeople. 26-Gate leading to the field. 27-Present gate. 28-29-Part of the line, made of yucca and stakes, which encloses the city. 30-31-32-33-Fresh water wells. Original in Archivo General de Indias.

troop retaliated by burning a few Apalachecola villages. What more could be done?

To Governor Torres belongs the credit for completing Castillo de San Marcos. Torres saw the last stones go into place for the water defenses—bright yellow coquina that was in strange contrast to weathered masonry almost a quarter of a century old. In August 1695 the workmen finally moved out of the Castillo. (Another job was waiting: a seawall that would keep storm tides out of the city.)

The pile of stone on which Cendoya planned to spend some 70,000 pesos and which Hita estimated would cost a good 80,000 if built elsewhere, now totaled at least 138,375 pesos, or about $220,000. And rather than the King's silver, it was the blood and sweat and hardship of the Florida soldier that paid the cost. For the money came out of his back pay, due but never collected by him of his heirs. Let the Castillo be his monument!

And what did completion of this citadel mean? Only a year later, soldiers gaunt with hunger slipped into the church and left an unsigned warning for the governor: If the enemy came, they intended to surrender, for they were starving.

Defending San Marcos

Castillo de San Marcos is a textbook design adapted to a frontier situation. It is a fortification style evolved from the medieval castle. Toward the end of the Middle Ages when the gunpowder cannon was invented, towering castle made fine targets for the artillerist. Stone walls that had turned aside the powerful bolt of the crossbow and resisted for days on end the slow pounding of the catapults tumbled into the rubble after a thundering siege from bombards and culverins.

So the engineers lowered their target-like walls, and in front of them they piled great hills of earth to stop the cannonballs before they could hit the stone. Yet, because those walls must yet be too high for the scaling ladders, the engineers kept their moats. The circular tower of the ancient castle evolved into the bastion, an angular, roomy salient from which pikemen, arquebusiers, and artillerists could see to defend all adjacent walls. The new fortification thus became a rather complicated series of straight walls and angles—a sort of defense-in-depth-plan—and in the center of it could usually be found the garrison quarters and the magazines.

For most defense problems there was an answer in the book, though the brilliance of the engineer might well be measured by his ingenious use of natural defenses, as achieved by Daza at Castillo de San Marcos. Fortification was, in fact, a remarkably exact science and one universally respected. "Many…argument," wrote an eighteenth-century expert, "might be alleged to prove the usefulness of fortified places, were it not that all the world is convinced of it at present, and therefore it would be needless to say more about." A fort, however, could never win a victory. It was a defensive weapon to protect vital points and delay the invader. And, as was the case with the historic fort in Florida, it could be a citadel and pivot of maneuver for colonial troops.

There were as many different kinds of forts as there were uses for them. They promoted and protected trade, they guarded the pass into a country, or, like San Marcos, they secured the country from invasion. The following dogma, written many years after the Castillo was started,

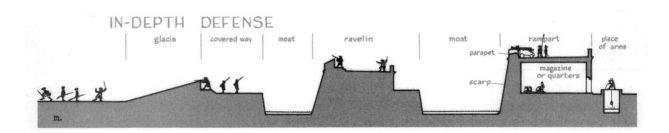

IN-DEPTH DEFENSE

glacis | covered way | moat | ravelin | moat | rampart | place of arms

parapet

scarp

magazine or quarters

m.

A gun crew preparing to fire on the British troops passing west of the Castillo, 1702.

might apply directly to the fort at St. Augustine: "In small states…which cannot afford the expense of building many fortresses, and are not able to provide them when built with sufficient garrisons and other necessaries for their defense, or those whose chief dependence consists in the protection of their allies; the best way is to fortify their capital, which being made spacious, may serve as a retreat to the inhabitants in time of danger, with their wealth and cattle, till the succours of their allies arrive."

To attack a seventeenth- or eighteenth-century fort, the enemy had first to cross natural barriers, advance over level ground exposed to fire from the fortification, drive the defenders from the outer works, cross the moat, and then (if there were any of him left) scale the main walls and fight the defenders hand to hand. It was not easy. His usual approach was to dig trenches for protection, and advance the trenches right up to the outworks.

Meanwhile, his artillerymen tried to get their guns close enough to breach the walls. Once he could bring his artillery to bear, the unfortunate defenders found themselves to be stationary targets subjected to devastating fire, particularly from the heavy mortars throwing 50- or 100-pound bombs into the confines of the fortification.

Most important of all, however, was food. The invading army was often far from its base and to some extent had to live off hostile country. But if the invader could isolate the fort, as he invariably tried to do, the siege lasted no longer than the food and water in the fort. For this reason, at least 5 of the 20 main rooms in Castillo de San marcos were for food storage, and three wells were dug in the courtyard. As long as the provision magazines were well filled, the citadel was strong.

The test of its strength was not long delayed. With France, there was peace again, but border animosities flamed high, fed by Indian rumors of an impending attack on St. Augustine itself by the Carolinians. Spain's Indian allies were restive, anxious to move out of the zone of conflict. And for good reason: the incursions by English-led Indians continued.

As tensions increased, Governor Jose de Zuniga y Cerda looked at the St. Augustine defenses with jaundiced eye. True the Castillo was a bulwark, but Zuniga knew, after a military career spanning 28 years (including the two-year siege of Melilla), that strong walls were not enough. Castillo guns were ancient and obsolete—many of them unserviceable. The powder from Nueva España so fouled the gun barrels that after "four shots, the Ball would not go in the Cannon." Arquebuses, muskets, powder, and shot were sorely needed.

Once again Captain Ayala sailed directly to Spain for aid. It was a race against time, for now it was 1702; England declared open war on Spain and France over the succession to the Spanish crown. Already Governor James Moore of Carolina was moving against St. Augustine. By snatching it out of Spain's hands, he would clap an English lock on the Bahama Channel and forestall Spanish-French designs on Charleston.

En route south, Moores' forces destroyed the Franciscan missions in the Guale country. At St. Augustine they swiftly by-passed the castillo and occupied the town. The people could do nothing but flee to the fort. South and west of its walls, where the outskirts of the town crept near, the Spanish burned many houses which could have hidden the enemy advance toward the fort.

Moore's 500 Englishmen and 300 Indians vastly outnumbered the 230 soldiers and 180 Indians and Negroes in the Spanish garrison, but he was ill-equipped to besiege the Castillo. He had only four cannon, and the Spanish boasted that continuous fire from the fort kept them out of range.

Moore settled down to await the arrival of more artillery from Jamaica, and thus matters stood when four Spanish men-of-war sailed from the south and blocked the harbor entrance, thus bottling up Moore's fleet of eight small vessels. He burned these ships, left many of his stores, and retreated overland to the St. Johns River. St. Augustine he left in ashes, but the Castillo survived the holocaust.

Damage to the town totalled 56,520 pesos,

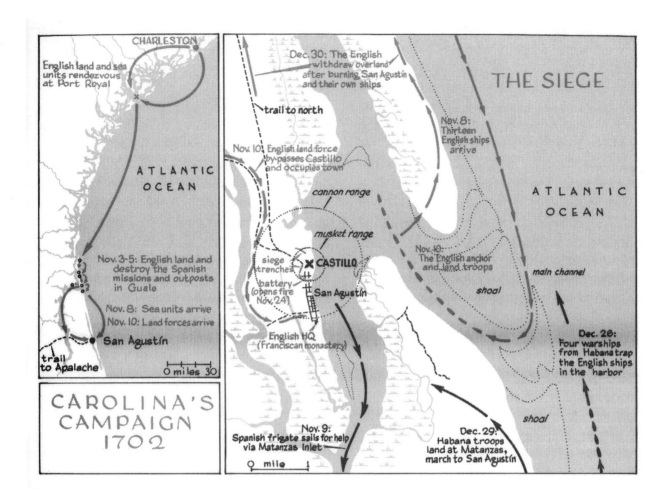

CAROLINA'S
CAMPAIGN
1702

THE SIEGE

and the ease with which the English had taken and held it for almost two months made it clear that more defenses were needed. Moreover, English-Indian obliteration of the missions in Apalache, Timucua and Guale had squeezed Spanish control down to the tiny mile-square area directly under the Castillo guns. This had to be held at any cost.

In the two decades that followed 1702, out from the Castillo went strong earthworks and palisades, buttressed at strategic points with redoubts. These made St. Augustine a walled town, secure against invasion as long as there were enough soldiers to man the walls. But in those dark days who could be sure of tomorrow? In 1712 came La Gran Hambre, the Great Hunger, when people ate even the dogs and cats.

The war ended at last in 1714. The hostile noose around St. Augustine slackened, but it was an uneasy kind of peace with many "incidents." In 1728 Colonel William Palmer of Carolina marched against the presidio. The grim

walls of the fort, the unwinking readiness of the heavy guns, and the needle-sharp points of the yucca plants lining the palisades were a powerful deterrent. Palmer "refrained" from taking the town. For their part, the Spaniards set off their artillery, but they made no sorties.

Palmer's bold foray to the very gates of St. Augustine foreshadowed a new move southward by the English, beginning with Savannah in 1732. With his eye on Florida, James Oglethorpe landed at St. Simons Island in 1736, built Fort Frederic, and nurtured it into a strong military post. From Frederica he pushed his Georgia boundary southward al the way to the St. Johns River—a scant 35 miles from St. Augustine. Meanwhile, Castillo de San Marcos began to show its half-century age and the palisades were rotting. That capable engineer and frontier diplomat, Antonio de Arrendondo, came from Habana to sound out the Georgians, inspect Florida's defenses, and make recommendations. Backed by Arredondo's expertise, Governor

Manuel de Montiano put all the cards on the table in a letter to the governor of Cuba, who had been made responsible for Florida's security: "Your Excellency must know that this castle, the only defense here, has no bombproofs for the protection of the garrison, that the counterscarp is too low, that there is no covered way, that the curtains are without demilunes, that there are no other exterior works to give them time for a long defense; …we are as bare outside as we are without life inside, for there are no guns that could last 24 hours and if there were, we have no artillerymen to serve them."

Cuba's governor was a resourceful administrator eager to meet his responsibility. He sent guns, soldiers, artisans, convicts, provisions and money. The walls would be heightened five feet and masonry vaults, to withstand English bombs, would replace the rotting beams of old rooms in the Castillo. Stronger outworks would be built. To supervise the project, Engineer Pedro Ruiz de Olano came from Venezuela. The work began in April 1738 rather inauspiciously. The master of construction, one Cantillo, was a syphilitic too sick to earn his 16-real daily wage. Much of his work fell to his assistant, a 12-real master mason. All six stonecutters were Negroes. One was an invalid, and none of them as yet had much skill with coquina. For moving stone, there was but one oxcart. The labor gang—52 convicts—was too small. Nevertheless, quarry and kiln hummed with activity, and in the Castillo the crash of demolition echoed as the convicts pulled down old rooms and began trenching for the new bombproofs. The start was on the east, because this side faced the inlet, where enemy action was likely to come first.

As usual, misfortunes beset the work. Cantillo's gálico worsened and Blas de Ortega came from Habana to replace him. Eight convicts on the limekiln deserted. Engineer Ruiz pulled off a crew of carpenters, sawyers, and axemen to rebuild a blockhouse where the trail to Apalache crossed the St. Johns.

The oxcart driver broke his arm. Quarrying and stonecutting dragged. The old quarry played

out. Luckily, a new one was found and opened, even though farther away. And Habana sent two more carts and more stonecutters and convicts. It was well into October before the carpenters began setting the forms for the vaults, but the masons soon moved in and finished the first of the massive, round-arched bombproofs before the year ended. By the next October all eight vaults, side by side along the east curtain, were done. Each one spanned a 17- by 34-foot area, and had its own door to the courtyard. Windows above and beside the door let in light and air.

The tops of the ponderous vaults were leveled off with a fill of coquina chips and sand. Tabby mortar was poured onto the surface, and tampers beat the mixture smooth. After the first layer set, another and another were added until the pavement was six inches thick. The whole roof was thus made into a gun deck, and cannon were no longer restricted to the bastions alone. For unlike the old raftered roof, the new terreplein was buttressed by construction that could take tremendous weight and terrific shock; and masonry four feet thick protected the rooms underneath from bombardment. In San Carlos bastion, by mid-January of 1740, they had finished the tall watchtower and the new parapet.

It was English progress in Georgia that had spurred all this activity. In fact, Spain's plan for recovery of Georgia and other Spanish-claimed land was well past the first stages. Troops were assembling in Habana and a reinforcement of 400 had already come to Florida. Actually, Florida-Georgia was only part of the knotty problem growing out of Spain's traditional policy: Spanish colonies shall trade only with Spanish ships. No foreigners! But if the Hispanic supply system broke down (as it often did), needy Spaniards welcomed foreign "aid", legal or not. Even after 1713, when Spain reluctantly gave England a trade concession, the quota was so small and the market so large that honest traders often became smugglers. Deciding who was honest was up to the coast guard. Since coast guard captures usually meant impressments of the crews and court condemnation of the vessels, Spain touched

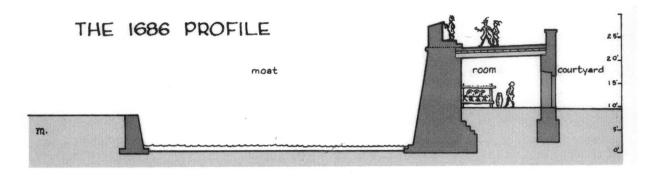

THE 1686 PROFILE

moat

room   courtyard

m.

England in two tender places—pride and pocketbook.

The man who sparked the war was Captain Robert Jenkins of the Rebecca. Jenkins told Parliament he was boarded off Florida, his ear sliced off and handed back by a Spanish officer who said: "Carry it to your King and tell his majesty that if he were present I would serve him in the same manner."

Pope, the couplet maker, smiled and said "the Spaniards did a waggish thing/Who cropped our ears and sent them to the King." But others were not amused, and England and Spain declared war in 1739. It was called, of course, the War of Jenkins' Ear.

England's main target was the Caribbean, with Habana at center and Porto Bello, Cartagena and St. Augustine on the perimeter. Admiral Vernon quickly won fame by his capture of Porto Bello (1739). James Oglethorpe would try to emulate him in Florida. Already he had probed the St. Johns River approaches, and St. Augustine would be next. Was the Castillo ready?

One English spy reported respectfully that "there is 22. pieces of Cannon well mounted on the Bastions from 6 pound'rs. To 36. they are very Cautious of the English & will not lett them go on the lines, there is a guard of a

Lieutenant a Serjeant & 2. Corporals & 30 Soldiers here who is relieved Every Day. There is one Lieutentant a Serjeant & 12. Gunners who is reliev'd once a Week, there is 5 Centries on ye lines at a time all Night, ye Man that is at the Bell Strikes it every 3. or 4. Minutes the Centry's Calling from one to the other…there is a Mote Round it of 30. foot wide & a draw Bridge of about 15 foot long, they draw every Night & Lett it down in the Morning…"

Governor Montiano, however, was fully aware of weaknesses. "Considering that 21 months have been spent on a bastion and eight arches," he pointed out, "we need at least eight years for rehabilitation of the Castillo." Of course, in making his case the governor did not see fit to mention that the crew had also built much of the Arrendondo-designed covered way and strengthened the earth wall from the Castillo west to the San Sebastian River.

But there was real reason for concern: work on the vaults had to stop as the war dried up construction funds. The fort was left in a strangely irregular shape. The east side, including San Carlos bastion, was at the new height, but all others were several feet lower. Old rooms still lined three sides of the courtyard.

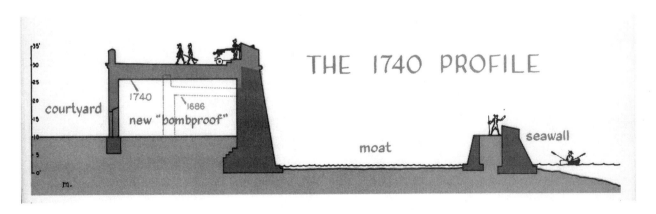

courtyard

1740

1686

new "bombproof"

THE 1740 PROFILE

moat   seawall

m.

The 1740 English Siege

On June 13, 1740 (by the Spanish calendar), seven British warships dropped anchor outside the inlet. The long-expected siege of St. Augustine was here. Montiano hastily sent the news to Habana and with it a plea for help. He had 750 soldiers and the 120 or more sailors who manned the galliots, but rations would be gone by the end of June.

The attackers numbered almost 1,400, including sailors and the Indian allies. While the warships blockaded the harbor on the east, William Palmer cme in from the north with a company of Highlanders and occupied the deserted outpost called Fort Mose. Oglethorpe landed his men and guns on each side of the inlet and began building batteries across the bay from the Castillo.

Montiano saw at once that all English positions were separated from each other by water, and could not speedily reinforce one another. Fort Mose, at the village of the black runaways a couple of miles north of the Castillo, was easily the weakest. At dawn on June 26 a sortie from St. Augustine hit Fort Mose, and in the bloodiest action of the siege scattered the Highlanders and burned the palisaded fortification. Colonel Palmer, that veteran of Florida campaigns, was among the dead.

As if in revenge, the siege guns at the inlet opened fire. Round shot whistled low over the bay and crashed into fort and town. Bombs from the mortars soared high—deadly dots against the bright summer sky—and fell swiftly to burst with terrific concussion. The townspeople fled,

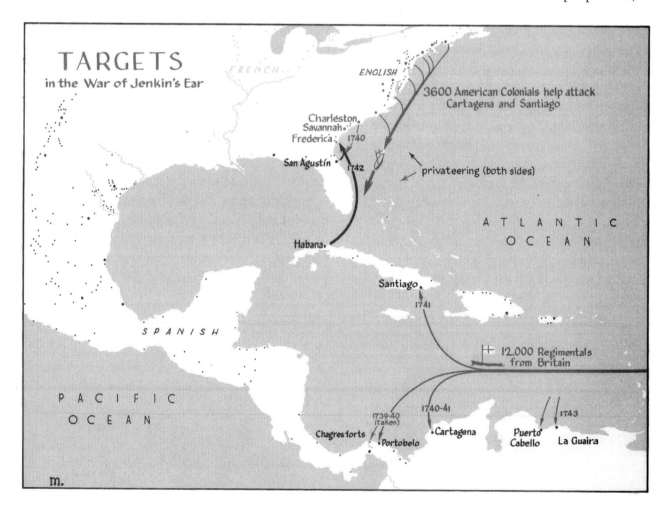

TARGETS
in the War of Jenkin's Ear

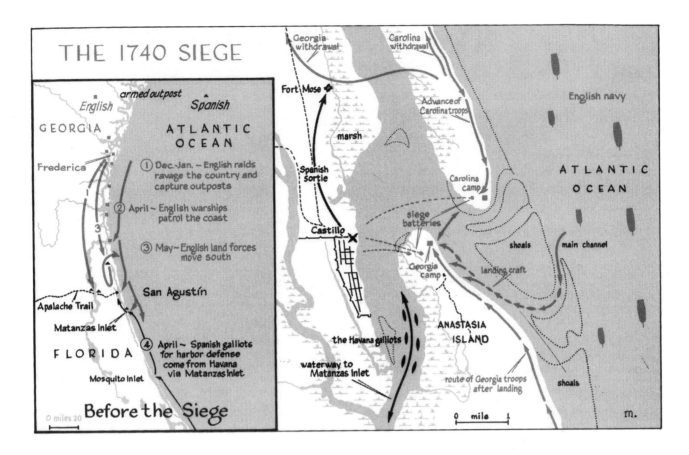

THE 1740 SIEGE

Before the Siege

English ▪ armed outpost ▲ Spanish

English
GEORGIA

ATLANTIC
OCEAN

Frederica

① Dec.-Jan. – English raids ravage the country and capture outposts

② April ~ English warships patrol the coast

③ May~ English land forces move south

San Agustín

Apalache Trail

Matanzas Inlet

FLORIDA

④ April ~ Spanish galliots for harbor defense come from Havana via Matanzas Inlet

Mosquito Inlet

0 miles 20

Georgia withdrawal

Carolina withdrawal

Fort Mose

marsh

Spanish sortie

Castillo

the Havana galliots

waterway to Matanzas Inlet

Advance of Carolina troops

Carolina camp

siege batteries

Georgia camp

shoals

main channel

landing craft

ANASTASIA ISLAND

route of Georgia troops after landing

shoals

English navy

ATLANTIC
OCEAN

0   mile   1

m.

2,000 of them, some to the woods, others to the covered way where Castillo walls screened them from the shelling.

For 27 nerve-shattering days the British batteries thundered. At the Castillo, newly laid stones in the east parapet scattered under the hits, but the weathered old walls held strong. As one Englishman observed, the native rock "will not splinter but will give way to cannon ball as though you would stick a knife into cheese." One of the balls shot away a gunner's leg, but only two men in the Castillo were killed in the bombardment.

The heavy guns of San Marcos and the long 9-pounders of the fast little galliots in the harbor kept the British back. Despite the bluster of the cannonades, the siege had stalemated. Astride the inlet, Oglethorpe and his men battled insects and shifting sand on barren, sun-baked shores, while Spanish soldiers in San Marcos, down to half rations themselves, saw their families and friends starving. On July 6 Montiano wrote, "My greatest anxiety is provisions. If these do not come, there is not

doubt that we shall die in the hands of hunger."

The very next day came news that supplies had reached a harbor down the coast south of Matanzas. Shallow-draft Spanish vessels went down the waterway behind Anastasia Island, fought their way out of Matanzas Inlet and, hugging the coast, went to fetch the provisions. Coming back into Matanzas that same night, they found the British blockader gone and reached St. Augustine unopposed.

Meanwhile, regardless of the low morale of his men, Oglethorpe made ready to assault the Castillo. His naval commander, however, was nervous over the approach of the hurricane season and refused to cooperate. Without support from the warships, Oglethorpe was beaten. Daybreak on the 38th day of the siege revealed—to Montiano's wondering relief—that the redcoats were gone.

43

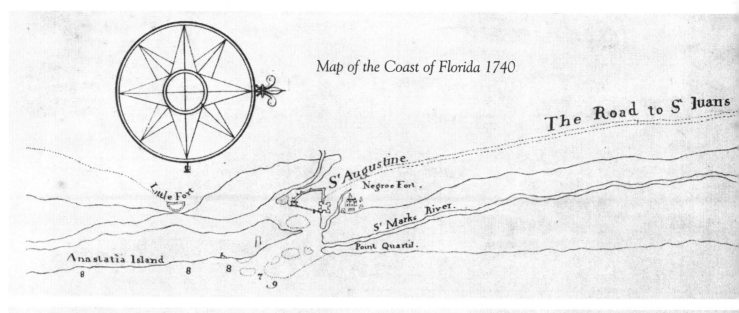

Map of the Coast of Florida 1740

The Road to St Juans

St Augustine.

Negroe Fort.

St Marks River.

Little Fort

Point Quartil.

Anastatia Island

8   8   8

7

9

EXPLANATION OR

A. The Town of St Augustine about one mile in lenght haveing a Rivulet around it.

B. The Castle L att by Observation. 29.59. N with water round it and a Drawbridge of Communication with the Town.

C. The River Matanxa its Entrance is at the Barr of Augustine.

D. The North part of the Island of Anastatia lying to the Eastward of the Town parted by the River Matxanxa ã a Mile in Breadth the West part of it is Marshland overflowed at Spring Tides the East part Sand. Hommocks and Palmetto Bushes.

E. St Marks River which runs almost to St Iohns River the Sº part of Georgia

F. Point Quartil where Coll Vanderduson first Pitched his Tents with the Carolina Soldiers

G. The North Chanel to Matanxa River

H. The North Breaker Shoals wt Part dry.

I. The South Breaker Shoul.

K. The Barr of Augustine the Entrance of the South Chanel which for its Shoalness Ships of Force cannot Enter.

L. The Place where General Oglethor landed with his Soldiers Sailors & Indians under Cover of the 20. Gun Ships without Opposition.

M. A Stake sand Battery Quitted.

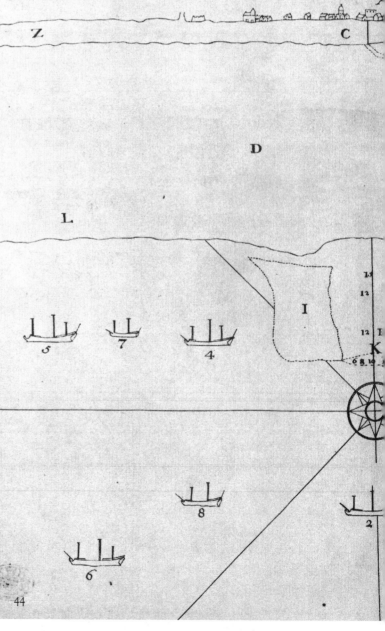

Map showing the postitions of the English during the siege of 1740

Z   C

D

L

5   7   4

I

K

H

8

6

2

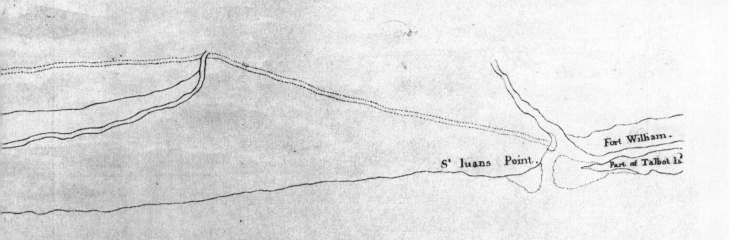

St luans Point.

Fort Wilham.

Part of Talbot Is.

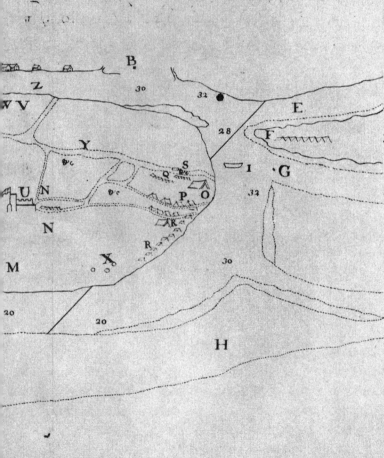

REFERENCES,

N.Quarrys of Stone.

O.The Generals Tent and main Guard.

P.The Sailors ....

Q.The Indians. } Tents.

R.The Carolina Soldiers.

S .A Battery of Sand Baggs with two 18. Pounders. and a Mortar w. 24.1.16.

T. A Sand Battery of Four 18 Pounders one 9 Pounder and 2 small Mortars ½ a Mile from the River.

U.The Lookout Quitted .

V.A Palmetto House and Cornfields to the Westward of which (on the Marsh) Twenty Cohorns play'd upon the Town .

W.The Place from which the Prospect of the Town and Castle was taken .

X .Wells dug by the Seamen to water their Shiping .

Y .The Sailors hawling Cannon in the Day time in reach of the Enemys Cannon .

Z.Galleys & half Galleys which Annoyd ÿ Forces

&c.Centinels of Soldiers.

1 .A Scooner Sloops and Periaugers Tenders to the General and Shiping .

2 .... { Flambrough .

3 .... Hector .

4.His Majestys Ships.{ Pheenix .

5 .... Squirrel .

6 .... Tartar.

7 .... { Spence .

8 His Majestys Sloops..{ Wolf .

This Coast is very subject in April. May and lune to squals. Rain.Thunder and Lightning and once in three years to Hurricanes .

The End of an Era

This was why the Castillo had been built—to resist the high tide of aggression, to stand firm through the darkest hour. It was the climax, the culmination of years of dogged labor and lean hunger. It was also the closing of an era, for the end was in sight. The clumsy Spanish reprisal in 1742, Oglethorpe's foolish return to St. Augustine the year following—these were the joustings of provincials uncertain of their destiny. Still, to the embattled actors on the scene, one thing seemed clear: the Castillo must be completed.

Despite the need to get back to work on the vaults, other projects were even more urgent. First came repair of the bombardment damage. After that, the defenses around fort and town were strengthened and a strong new earth wall called the hornwork was thrown up across the land approach, half a mile north of town. And for a year or more a sizable crew was busy at Matanzas building a permanent tower and battery, since 1740 had again shown the vital importance of this inlet.

Thus several years slipped by and at the Castillo itself—the heart of the defense system—nothing was done. Termites and rot were in the old rafters and in 1749 part of the roof collapsed.

The governor's appeal to the crown eventually brought action. Engineer Pedro de Brozas y Garay came from Ceuta (Africa) to replace Ruiz, who was returning to Spain. And, having erected the rest of the fort rooms, it was Brozas who, with Governor Alonso Fernandez de Heredia, stood under the royal coat of arms at the sally port as the masons set in the inscription giving credit to the governor and himself for completion of the Castillo in 1756. The ceremony was a politic gesture, carried out on the name day of King Fernando VI; but in truth there was still a great deal to do.

The new bombproof vaults had raised Castillo walls by five feet. Where once they had measured about 25 feet from foundation to crown of parapet, now they were above 30. The little ravelin of 1683 could no longer shield the main gate, and as yet the covered way screened only the base of the high new walls. The glacis existed only in plan.

So, having finished the vaults, the builders moved outside and worked until money ran out in the spring of 1758. The break lasted until 1762, by which time Britain and Spain were again at war. Spain, as an ally of France, got into the fracas just at the time when Britain had eliminated France as a factor in the control of North America, and was quite ready to take on Spain. And this time the British would capture the pearl of the Antilles—Habana itself.

Habana was well fortified and the board of general officers sitting there, not being prescient, were perhaps more worried over St. Augustine than Habana. They released 10,000 pesos for strengthening of Florida fortifications and sent Engineer Pablo Castello to assist ailing Pedro Brozas. Castello had been teaching mathematics at the military college in Habana.

St. Augustine had only 25 convicts for labor, but as work began on July 27, 1762, many soldiers and townspeople sensed the urgency—Habana was already under siege—and volunteered to help. Since much of the project was a simple but manpower-consuming task of digging and moving a mountain of sand from borrow pit to earthwork, all hands with a strong back were welcome. The volunteers did, in fact, contribute labor worth more than 12,000 pesos. The only paid workers were the teamsters driving the 50 horses that hauled the fill. Each dray dumped 40 cubic feet of earth, and the hauling kept on until the covered way had been raised five more feet to its new height.

The masons soon finished a stone parapet, six feet high, for the new covered way. With this wall in place, the teamsters moved outside the covered way and began dumping fill for the

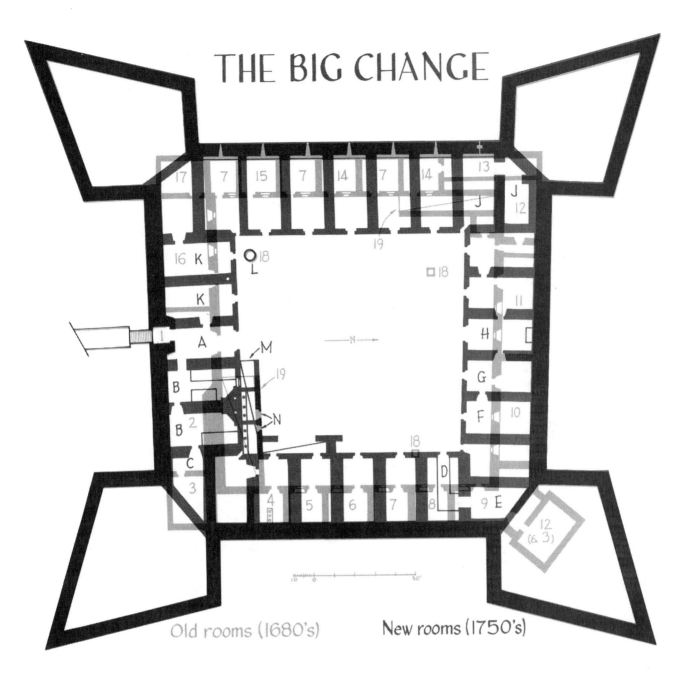

Old rooms (1680's)   New rooms (1750's)

Key: 1-sally port. 2-guardroom. 3-prision. 4-latrine. 5-smithy. 6-overseer. 7-provisions. 8-kitchen. 9-ordnance supplies. 10-ration distribution. 11-subsidy supplies from New Spain. 12-magazine. 13-ship supplies. 14-arms. 15-commandant quarters. 16-chapel. 17-sacristy. 18-wells. 19-ramps. A-sally port. B-guardrooms and kitchens. C-prison. D-gunners' quarters. E-ordnance supplies. F-treasury. G-accountant. H-chapel. J-magazines. K-officers' quarters. L-well. M-ramp. N-latrines. Others: storerooms.

glacis. This simple but important structure was a carefully designed slope from the field up to the parapet of the covered way. Not only would it screen the main walls and covered way, but its upward slope would lift attackers right into the sights of the fort cannon.

Meanwhile, to replace the 1682 ravelin, Castello began a new one with room for five cannon and a powder magazine. He realigned the moat wall to accommodate the larger work and pushed the job along so that as December of 1762 ended, the masons laid the final stone of the cordon for the ravelin. They never started its parapet. For also the close of the year brought the wrenching news that Spain would give Florida to Great Britain.

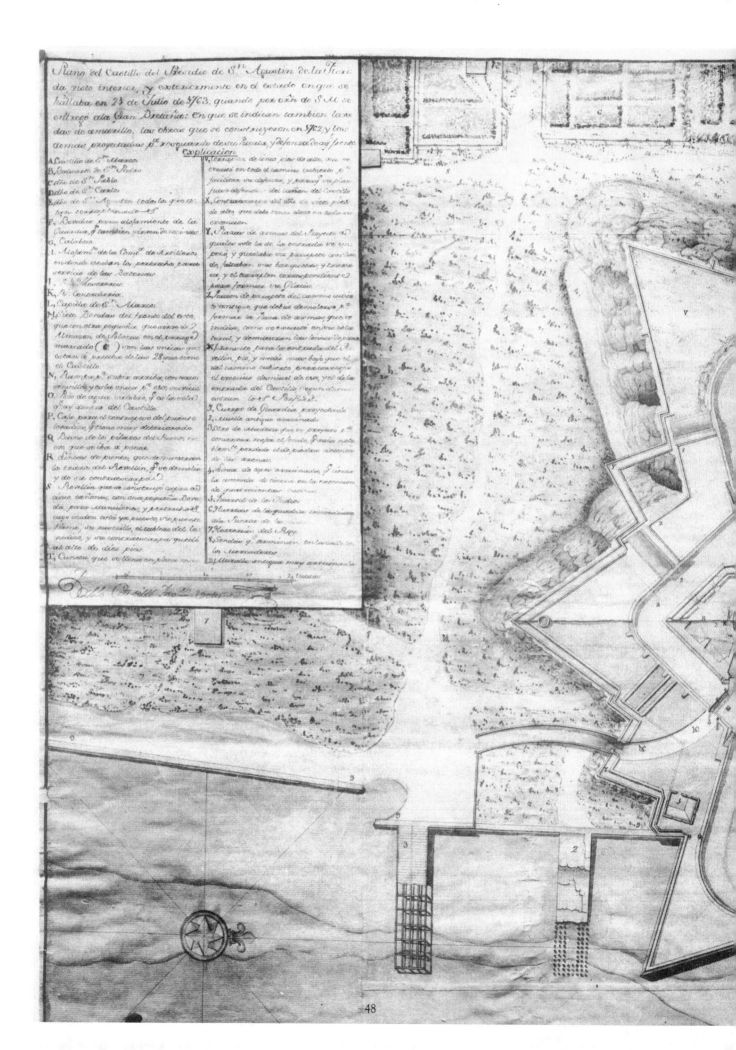

49

English Period 1763

So Spain's work on the fort ended. And although ravelin and glacis were not finished, Castillo de San Marcos was a handsome structure. The main walls were finished with a hard, waterproofing, lime plaster, shining white in the sunlight with the brilliance of Spain's olden glory. In the haste of building, engineers had not forgotten such niceties as classic molded cornices, pendants and pilasters to cast relieving shadow on stark smooth walls. At the point of each bastion was color—the tile-red plaster of the sentry boxes. White and red. These were Spain's symbolic colors, revealed again in the banner floating above the ramparts.

With walls high over the blue water of the bay, its towers thrusting toward the clouds, and guns of bright bronze or iron pointed over turf and sweep of marsh toward the gloom of the forest or the distant surf racing on the bar, San Marcos was properly the background for Florida's capital. In the narrow streets that led to the citadel, military men mingled with tradesmen and townsfolk. Sailors were here, for to this city the sea was life. Indians, people of the woodland continent, their nakedness smeared with beargrease against the bugs, were a strange contrast to the silken opulence of the governor's lady. But this was St. Augustine—a town of contrasts, with a long past and an uncertain future.

Great Britain, having possession of Habana and certain other advantages, dictated the peace terms of 1763. She chose to acquire Florida. A vast wilderness with military settlements at St. Augustine and Pensacola, the land had been coveted by generations of English colonials not only because it lay beside the sea lanes, but for its Indian trade and giant forests of pine and live oak needful to a shipbuilding people. Too, this southerly clime gave promise to thriving sugar and indigo plantations.

The day of the transfer was July 21, 1763. At Castillo de San Marcos, Governor Melchor de Feliu delivered the keys to Major John Hedges, at the moment the ranking representative of George III. The Spanish troops departed Florida, and with them went the entire Spanish population. The English were left with an empty city.

The defenses they found at St. Augustine were far stronger than the ones that had stopped Oglethorpe in 1740. The renovated Castillo (which the new owners called Fort St. Mark) was the citadel of a defense-in-depth system which began with fortified towers at St. Augustine and Matanzas inlets and blockhouses at the St. Johns River crossings. Since St. Augustine was on a small peninsula with Matanzas Bay on one side and the San Sebastian River on the other, there was only one way to reach the city by land; and Fort Mose, rebuilt and enlarged after 1740, guarded this lone access. In 1762 Mose also became the anchor for a mile-long defense line across the peninsula to a strong redoubt on the San Sebastian. This earthwork, planted at its base with the spiny yucca so aptly named "Spanish bayonet," protected the essential farmlands behind it. Just north of the Castillo, the hornwork spanned the narrowest part of the peninsula. A third line stretched from the Castillo to the San Sebastian, and this one was intersected by a fourth line that enclosed the town on west and south. Along the eastern shore was the stone seawall. One by one, these defenses had evolved in the years following 1702.

Such defensive precautions seemed outmoded, now that all of eastern North America was under one sovereignty. Obviously the old enemies between Florida and the English colonies had departed with the Spaniards; Britain saw no need for concern about the fortifications. No need, that is, until the Thirteen Colonies showed disquieting signs of rebellion. And as rebellion flamed into

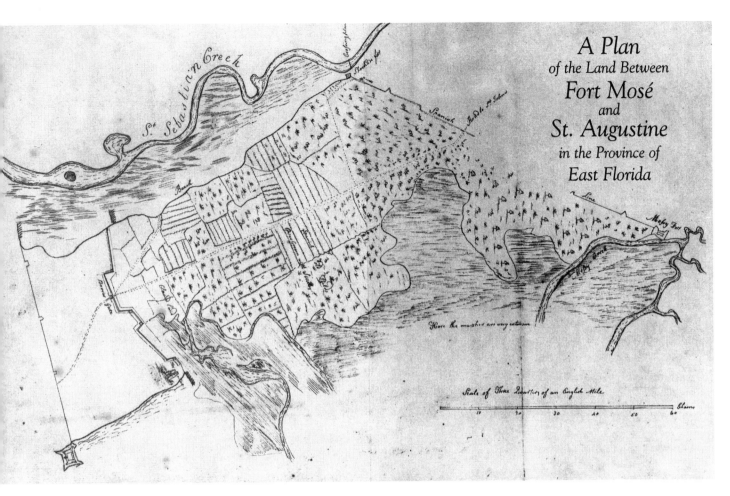

A Plan
of the Land Between
Fort Mosé
and
St. Augustine
in the Province of
East Florida

revolution among the Thirteen, St. Augustine entered a new role as capital of King George's loyal province of East Florida. Perhaps the defenses might be needed after all!

In the summer of 1775, after Lexington and Concord, the Castillo began to show the marks of British concern. The gate was repaired and the well in the courtyard, which had become brackish, was re-dug. In several of the high-arched bombproofs, the carpenters doubled the capacity by building a second floor, for St. Augustine was regimental headquarters and many redcoated troops were quartered in Fort St. Mark.

By October 1776, the British had renovated two of the three lines constructed north of the city by the Spanish. In place of the old earthwork that hemmed in the town on the south and west, however, they depended on a pair of detached redoubts at the San Sebastian, one at the ford and the other at the ferry. Later they added five other redoubts in the same

quadrant.

Across the covered way the engineers raised in 1779-80 several traverses—breastworks to stop enfilade fire from attackers; for better protection of the northwest bastion and the north curtain; they built an earthwork bonnet and a counterguard in the covered way; and on the east they strengthened the covered way salients by adding several feet to the thickness of the parapets. The glacis was also improved.

Within the safety of the thick walls were stored the arms that went to ranger, regular, and Indian ally alike for repeated use against the rebellious colonials to the north. And a goodly number of those colonials and their friends languished in the damp prison of the castle.

With the Castillo in English hands, yet armed against Georgia and Carolina (Spanish Florida's old foes), perhaps it would have been the final irony if the Spaniards had carried out their plan to capture St. Augustine. Indeed, the plan was complete down to the last detail:

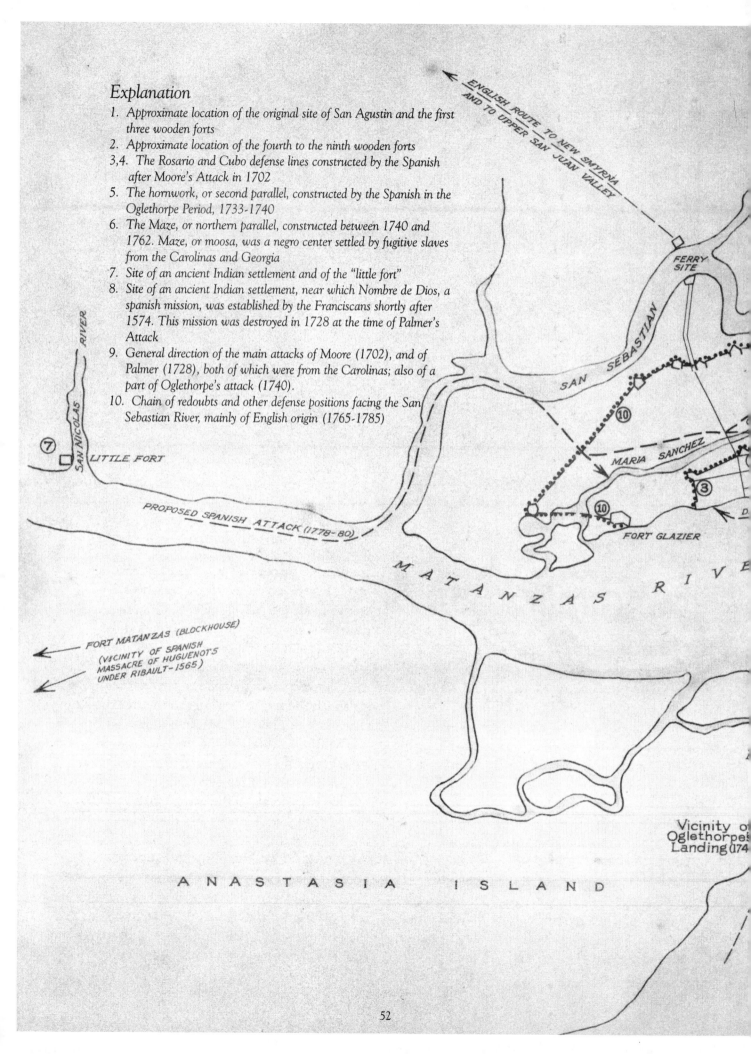

Explanation

1. *Approximate location of the original site of San Agustin and the first three wooden forts*
2. *Approximate location of the fourth to the ninth wooden forts*
3,4. *The Rosario and Cubo defense lines constructed by the Spanish after Moore's Attack in 1702*
5. *The hornwork, or second parallel, constructed by the Spanish in the Oglethorpe Period, 1733-1740*
6. *The Maze, or northern parallel, constructed between 1740 and 1762. Maze, or moosa, was a negro center settled by fugitive slaves from the Carolinas and Georgia*
7. *Site of an ancient Indian settlement and of the "little fort"*
8. *Site of an ancient Indian settlement, near which Nombre de Dios, a spanish mission, was established by the Franciscans shortly after 1574. This mission was destroyed in 1728 at the time of Palmer's Attack*
9. *General direction of the main attacks of Moore (1702), and of Palmer (1728), both of which were from the Carolinas; also of a part of Oglethorpe's attack (1740).*
10. *Chain of redoubts and other defense positions facing the San Sebastian River, mainly of English origin (1765-1785)*

ENGLISH ROUTE TO NEW SMYRNA
AND TO UPPER SAN JUAN VALLEY

FERRY SITE

SAN SEBASTIAN

SAN NICOLAS RIVER

⑦ LITTLE FORT

⑩

MARIA SANCHEZ

③

⑩

FORT GLAZIER

PROPOSED SPANISH ATTACK (1778-80)

M A T A N Z A S   R I V E

FORT MATANZAS (BLOCKHOUSE)
(VICINITY OF SPANISH MASSACRE OF HUGUENOTS UNDER RIBAULT-1565)

Vicinity of
Oglethorpe's
Landing (174

A N A S T A S I A   I S L A N D

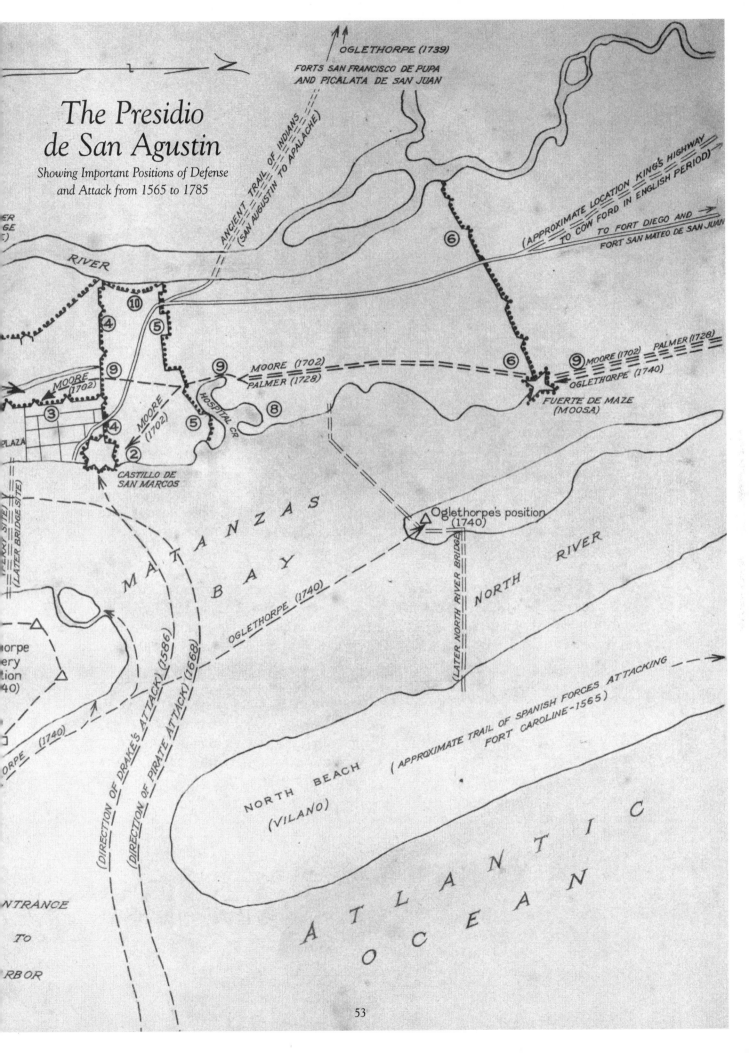

The Presidio de San Agustin

Showing Important Positions of Defense and Attack from 1565 to 1785

OGLETHORPE (1739)

FORTS SAN FRANCISCO DE PUPA
AND PICALATA DE SAN JUAN

ANCIENT TRAIL OF INDIANS
(SAN AUGUSTIN TO APALACHE)

(APPROXIMATE LOCATION KING'S HIGHWAY
TO COW FORD IN ENGLISH PERIOD)

TO FORT DIEGO AND
FORT SAN MATEO DE SAN JUAN

RIVER

⑩

④ ⑤

⑥

⑨ MOORE (1702) PALMER (1728)
OGLETHORPE (1740)

MOORE (1702)
PALMER (1728) ⑨

⑥

FUERTE DE MAZE
(MOOSA)

MOORE
(1702)

⑧

③

④ MOORE
(1702) ⑤

PLAZA

②

CASTILLO DE
SAN MARCOS

HOSPITAL CR.

(FERRY SITE)
(LATER BRIDGE SITE)

M A T A N Z A S   B A Y

Oglethorpe's position
(1740)

N O R T H   R I V E R

LATER NORTH RIVER BRIDGE

OGLETHORPE (1740)

horpe
ery
tion
40)

ORPE (1740)

(DIRECTION OF DRAKE'S ATTACK) (1586)

(DIRECTION OF PIRATE ATTACK) (1668)

(APPROXIMATE TRAIL OF SPANISH FORCES ATTACKING
FORT CAROLINE - 1565)

NTRANCE

TO

RBOR

NORTH BEACH
(VILANO)

A T L A N T I C
O C E A N

53

Printed for W. Faden Charing Cross.

ST. AUGUSTINE

the CAPITAL *of*

EAST FLORIDA.

SCALE,
660 Feet or 1 Furlong.

troops would come upriver from Matanzas, debark south of town, sweep northward through the city, and take the Castillo by surprise and escalade. If the assault failed, they would settle down to a siege. But the board of generals decided to strike Pensacola first. After all, the Castillo was no easy target—even in the hands of Englishmen!

Those were exciting times, but they were only an interlude. The British ensign was not the flag for the fort, and by the terms of the 1783 treaty, the Spanish came back on July 12, 1784.

Spanish Return 1783

They came back to an impossible situation. The border problems of earlier times were multiplied as runaway slaves from Georgia found welcome among the Seminole Indians, and ruffians from both land and sea made Florida their habitat.

Bedeviled by these perversities and distracted by revolutionary unrest in Latin America, Spain nevertheless did what had to be done at the Castillo: repairs to the bridges, a new pine stairway for San Carlos tower, a bench for the criminals in the prison. In 1785 Mariano de la Rocque designed an attractive entrance in

the neoclassic style for the chapel doorway. It was built, only to crumble slowly away like the Spanish hold on Florida.

Defense concepts were changed somewhat from earlier times. The British had built a few redoubts to cover vulnerable approaches on the west and south. The Spaniards on their return adapted the British works but also greatly strengthened the long wall from the Castillo to the San Sebastian. They widened its moat to 40 feet, lined the entire length of the 9-foot-high earthwork with palm logs, and planted it with Spanish bayonet. Its three redoubts were armed with light cannon.

And in this log wall a new city gate was completed in 1808. Its twin towers of white masonry were trimmed with red plaster, and each roof was capped with a pomegranate, a symbol of fertility.

Even though San Marcos remained a bulwark that American advances during this troublous period never quite reached, Florida had lost its old importance to Spain. One by one her colonies had slipped away into independence. Perhaps Spanish officials signed the papers ceding Florida to the United States with a sigh of relief, glad to be rid of a province so burdensome and unprofitable for 300 years.

THE CHANGE of FLAGS ~ JULY 10ᵀᴴ 1821

On July 10, 1821 the flag of Spain came down to the thunderous salute of Castillo cannon, and up went the 23-star flag of the United States of America.

American Territory 1821

So on July 10, 1821 the ensign of Spain came down to the thunderous salute of Castillo cannon, and up went the 23-star flag of the United States of America.

Although physically imposing, the proud Castillo de San Marcos continued to serve as an impressive reminder of Spain's past glories. The arrival of the Americans brought with it dramatic changes in the role the fortress would play. Renamed Fort Marion, the Castillo that had once protected an important outpost of Imperial Spain was assigned the more mundane duties of prison, storehouse, and inevitably, tourist destination.

In fact, the early days of American administration brought with it perhaps the greatest threats ever posed to the Castillo's survival. The removal of stones from the seawall to build a wharf brought with it dire consequences - seawater gradually flooded into the moat and began to eat away at Fort Marion's foundation. In 1834, storms and associated high tides brought further deterioration - damage so severe that local residents successfully appealed to the U.S. Army Corps of Engineers and critical repairs were made to save the fort

In 1837, two separate incidents in which the U.S. Army violated one of the oldest customs of warfare by capturing enemies who approached under a white flag of truce, resulted in the capture of Osceola and several of his lieutenants. Osceola, in failing health, was moved to South Carolina where he died at Fort Moultrie on January 31, 1838.

In 1842, the Second Seminole War was brought to a quiet conclusion and tourists once more felt safe about traveling to the Ancient City where they could gaze upon what remained of an exotic Spanish past, a bygone era that was symbolized by the mighty fortress now known as

Osceola

When the news of secession reached St. Augustine, the Governor of the State ordered that the fort, the barracks, and Federal property be taken possession of. Just a year into the conflict, Confederate forces abandoned Fort Marion in St. Augustine. On March 11, 1862, the Union gunboat, U.S.S. Wabash, took the fort without firing a shot. Local officials agreed to surrender the historic city in an attempt to save it from destruction. For the remainder of the Civil War, the fort served as a military installation occupied by Union troops. Florida, the least populous state below the Mason-Dixon line, played an active role in the Civil War. An estimated 16,000 Floridians fought in the conflict and the state's coastline provided safe harbor to blockade runners. Florida products—sugar, pork, molasses and salt—proved essential in feeding Southern soldiers. Both photographs of Union troops by Samuel A. Cooley, December 1864, Library of Congress.

Fort Marion. No visit to St. Augustine was complete without a stroll past the ageless battlements of the impressive guardian of the city and its harbor. As more and more Americans came to the oldest city to experience the past, to flee the chill of northern winters, or to recover from a host of maladies, the fort became the most memorable and enduring symbol of their visit to St. Augustine.

The fort's military attributes were once more put to good use in 1861 at the opening of the Civil War. As the headquarters for Confederate military operations in what remained a somewhat isolated part of America's southern frontier, a small expedition was dispatched from the fort with the task of extinguishing lighthouses along Florida's Atlantic coastline. Fort Marion's service to the Confederacy soon ended, however, in March of 1862 when a Union gunboat arrived to demand the town's surrender. In sharp contrast to the battles of long ago, the fort and the town were relinquished to the Northern invader without a shot being fired in their defense. For the

remainder of the conflict, the fort served as a largely forgotten military installation occupied by rear guard Union troops who seemed content to simply enjoy the warmth of the Florida sun.

By 1875, the Castillo had returned to its role as a place of incarceration for Native Americans. This time it wasn't the Florida Seminoles who were imprisoned within the ancient coquina walls. Instead, the inmates were now from the distant Great Plains and included Cheyenne, Arapaho, Comanche, and Kiowa. For the most part, these prisoners were men who had refused to accept the Federal government's system of reservations for controlling the once-proud tribes. Fortunately for these former warriors of the Plains, Captain Richard Pratt was their jailer. Under his direction, the prisoners not only learned English, they were allowed to sell handmade trinkets to tourists and even entertained guests at local hotels by performing authentic dances and demonstrating their archery skills. Next, Pratt developed courses for teaching job skills and professional trades to his prisoners. Inspired by

St. Augustine Historical Society

The Castillo became a place of incarceration for Native Americans. The prisoners shown here were Plains Indians from the Southwest whose presence in St. Augustine became a major tourist attraction

the results, he went on to create the famous Carlisle Indian School in Pennsylvania.

The upper deck of the Castillo took on a entirely new look in 1886 when it was crowded with tents erected to house the latest Native Americans made prisoner by the U.S. Army. This time, the prisoners were notorious Apaches from the Southwest whose presence in St. Augustine became a major tourist attraction – especially the three women who claimed to be wives of the infamous Geronimo. For Pratt, these prisoners also represented an ideal source of students for his Indian School.

In 1885 when millionaire Henry Flagler drew up his plans for transforming St. Augustine into an exclusive winter getaway for America's wealthiest families, he was staying just across the street from the Castillo at the San Marco Hotel. For Flagler, the Castillo represented a major selling point for his resort – its antiquity and authentic link to Spanish conquistadores, pirates, and the romantic appeal of a by-gone era were unique attributes that potential visitors found hard to resist. In typical Flagler fashion,

another tourism entrepreneur eventually combined the past and the present when he created a popular golf course on the Castillo's grounds, the first golf course in Florida.

The Castillo's transition from military installation to tourist attraction was solidified after the Great Fire of 1914 swept through the town. Among the losses from the fire were the collections of the St. Augustine Historical Society. In response to a Society appeal, the U.S. War Department granted permission for the group to use the Castillo as their headquarters. Within a matter of weeks, the Society was conducting tours from the Castillo. In 1924, with the Historical Society's strong support and work, the Castillo was designated as a national landmark. In 1933, the Castillo's long military service came to an end with the passage of the Historic Sites Act. Under the terms of this legislation, the U.S. War Department transferred its responsibility for administering the Castillo to the National Park Service.

In 1942, the Park Service abandoned the name "Fort Marion" and re-instated its original

When noted artist and wildlife enthusiast John James Audubon visited in 1832, his written impressions of the town were somewhat less than generous. Yet, he chose the Castillo as the backdrop for one of his famous bird paintings - "Greenshank".

In 1885 millionaire Henry Flagler drew up his plans for transforming St. Augustine into an exclusive winter getaway for America's wealthiest families. Another tourism entrepreneur eventually combined the past and the present when he created a popular golf course on the Castillo's grounds. It was the first golf course in Florida.

name – Castillo de San Marcos—a lasting tribute to the men and women for whom the existence of the Castillo had truly meant the difference between life and death.

In this new era, the aging fort was already a relic. The strategy of St. Augustine Harbor was gone. The young United States built powerful seacoast forts from Maine to Texas but at this one-time capital of the Southeast the engineers added only a water battery in the east moat (1842-44), mounted a few new guns on the bastions, and improved the glacis.

The fort was little changed, except in name. The Americans chose to honor General Francis Marion, Revolutionary leader and son of the very colony against which San Marcos had been built, so in 1825 Castillo de San Marcos became Fort Marion. Congress restored the original name in 1942.

Heavy doors and iron bars that once protected precious stores of food and ammunition made the old fort a good prison, and the prison days soon obscured the olden times when Spain's hold upon Florida depended upon the strength of these walls and the brave hearts who manned them. For by now the echo of the Spanish tongue had faded and the scarred walls were silent, their history hidden in faraway archives.

Small wonder that such things as a "secret dungeon" had to be invented! Accidental discovery of an obsolete magazine, walled up during the modernization of 1738-1739, was garnished with a Gothic plot—a tale of young lovers sealed into a tomb by a flint-hearted father. Such fictional romancings are not worthy of the Castillo, for in the documents one reads far better stories which, if a bit less macabre, have the virtue of being true and genuinely moving accounts of human suffering and achievement.

Crossing the language barrier into Castillo history gives new insight into the age-old misunderstandings between Spaniard and Englishmen. The records tell of the people who built and defended the Castillo—and those who attacked it, too. In the archives are countless instances of unselfish zeal and loyalty, the cases of Ransom, Collins, and Carr, the crown's patriarchal protection of its Indian vassals, the unflagging work of the friars.

True, there have been some, even in early times, who could see past the blackness of the dungeon, who did not need the written word to perceive the essence of this landmark. Such a one was William Cullen Bryant. "The old fort of St. Mark," he wrote, "is a noble work, frowning over the Matanzas, and it is worth making a long journey to see."

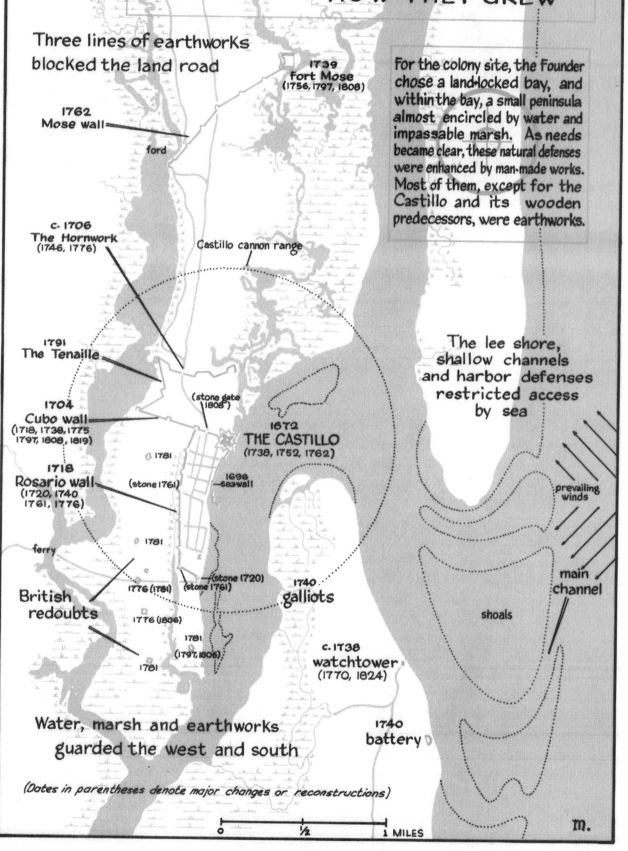

THE DEFENSES
– HOW THEY GREW

Three lines of earthworks
blocked the land road

1739
Fort Mose
(1756, 1797, 1808)

For the colony site, the Founder
chose a land-locked bay, and
within the bay, a small peninsula
almost encircled by water and
impassable marsh. As needs
became clear, these natural defenses
were enhanced by man-made works.
Most of them, except for the
Castillo and its wooden
predecessors, were earthworks.

1762
Mose wall

ford

c. 1706
The Hornwork
(1746, 1776)

Castillo cannon range

1791
The Tenaille

The lee shore,
shallow channels
and harbor defenses
restricted access
by sea

(stone gate
1808)

1704
Cubo wall
(1718, 1738, 1775
1797, 1808, 1819)

1672
THE CASTILLO
(1738, 1752, 1762)

prevailing
winds

1781

(stone 1761)

1718
Rosario wall
(1720, 1740
1761, 1776)

1698
seawall

ferry

1781

main
channel

1740
galliots

(stone 1720)
(stone 1761)

British
redoubts

1776 (1781)

shoals

1776 (1806)

1781
(1797, 1806)

c. 1738
watchtower
(1770, 1824)

1781

Water, marsh and earthworks
guarded the west and south

1740
battery

(Dates in parentheses denote major changes or reconstructions)

0   ½   1 MILES

m.

60

Bayoneta
bayonet

Casaca
greatcoat

Cartuchera
cartridge box

Trapilla
garter

Botones
buttons

Camisa
shirt

Cartuchera
cartridge box

Chupa
waistcoat

Polainas
leggins/gaiters

Fusil
musket

Sombrero Tricornio
tricorn hat

Vuelta/ Buelta
cuff

Escarapela
cockade

Corbata de Lazada
cravat

Casaca
greatcoat

Birial/ Cinturon
sword belt

Espada
sword

Bolsillo
pocket flap

Calzón
breeches

Medias
stockings

Zapatos
shoes

GLOSSARY

The following terms are defined as specifically used in this book. Some of them of course have other meanings, which are not applicable here.

Arquebus—Portable firearm invented about 1450, having a matchlock operated by a trigger. (See match.)

Bastion—A 4-sided salient which projects from the scarp of a fort. The bastion was developed in Italy about 1450.

Bomb—A shell, or hollow iron ball filled with explosive and fired from a mortar. Its detonation was timed by a powder fuze.

Bombproof—A room built to resist destruction by bombardment; a shelter from bombshells.

Bonnet—A cap, or V-shaped work, raised in front of a fortification salient to shield it from frontal fire.

Caballero—(Sp.) A cavalier, i. e., a raised platform inside a fort, giving the defender's cannons the advantage of elevation over attacking forces.

Cordon—The ornamental projecting course of stone where the parapet wall joins the scarp.

Counterguard—A detached, narrow rampart placed in front of an important wall to prevent fire from breaching it.

Counterscarp—The wall opposite the scarp; the moat wall.

Covered way—The area between the moat and the exterior embankment (glacis), protected or "covered" from enemy fire by this embankment.

Curtain—The wall connecting two bastions, i. e., part of the scarp or main wall of the fort.

Embrasure—An opening in a wall or parapet, through which cannon are fired.

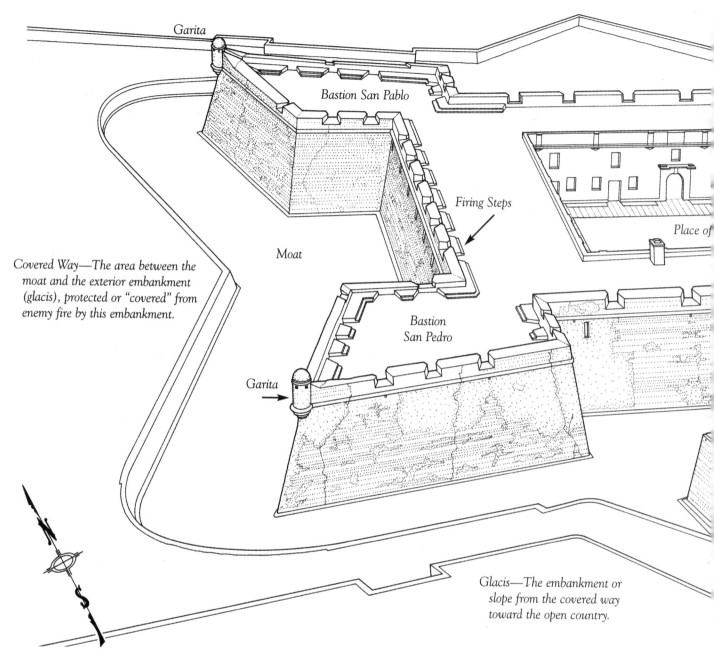

Garita

Bastion San Pablo

Firing Steps

Place of

Covered Way—The area between the moat and the exterior embankment (glacis), protected or "covered" from enemy fire by this embankment.

Moat

Bastion
San Pedro

Garita

Glacis—The embankment or slope from the covered way toward the open country.

N
S

Enfilade—To rake the length of a target with gunfire.

Escalade—The act of climbing the walls of a fortification by ladders.

Firing step—The raised step or bank along the inside of a parapet, on which soldiers are posted to fire upon the enemy.

Galliot—Small, swift galley, using both sails and oars.

Gate—Entrance; sallyport.

Glacis—The embankment or slope from the covered way toward the open country.

Gorge—The throat or entrance into a bastion.

Gunner's ladle—A copper scoop fixed to a pole and used for measuring powder and loading it into a cannon.

Hornwork—An earthwork having a curtain and two half-bastions. Its plan resembles the projecting horns of a bull.

Match—A wick or cord chemically prepared to burn at uniform rate, for firing a charge of powder.

Mortar—Short cannon used for firing shells at a high angle, as lobbing them over the walls of a fort into the courtyard.

Musket—The smooth-bore predecessor of the rifle. Invented about 1540, it was more powerful than the arquebus, which it superseded.

Nueva España—(New Spain)—México.

Pale—A pointed stake. Pales were set vertically into the ground or fastened to rails as fencing.

Palisade—A high fence or barricade of pole timbers set vertically into the ground in a close row as a means of defense.

Parapet—A wall raised above the main wall or rampart of the fort to protect the defenders from attacking fire.

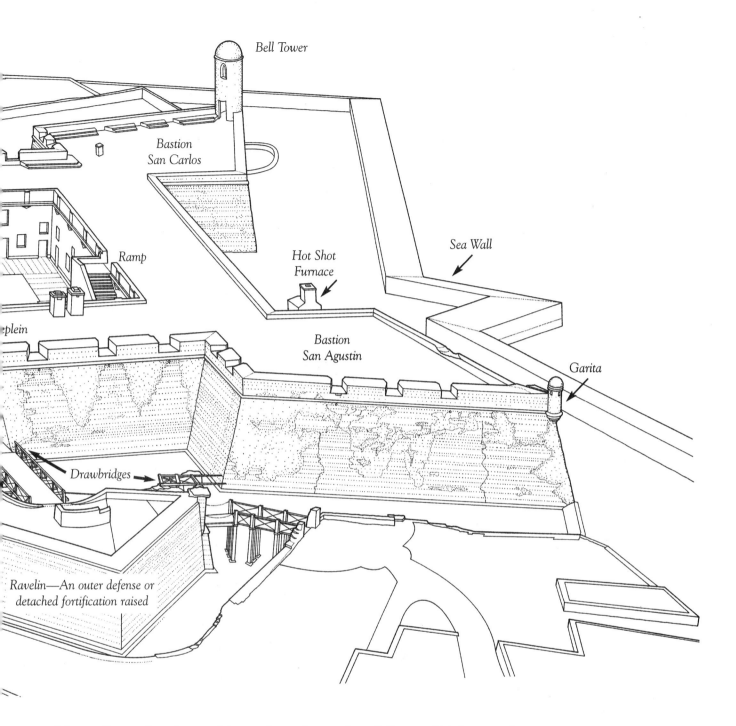

Bell Tower

Bastion
San Carlos

Ramp

Hot Shot
Furnace

Sea Wall

Bastion
San Agustin

Garita

eplein

Drawbridges

Ravelin—An outer defense or
detached fortification raised

Pilaster—Rectangular column with base and capital, inserted
  into a wall, but projecting outward about a quarter of its width.
Piragua—A canoe made of a hollowed tree trunk.
Portcullis—A grating to close the entrance of a fortification.
Postern—A small rear gate.
Presidio—(Sp.) A fortified settlement.
Rammer—A pole having a wooden head for ramming home
  the projectile or the charge of a cannon.
Rampart—The main body of a fortification around a place, on
  which the parapet is raised.
Ravelin—An outer defense or detached fortification raised
  before a curtain, especially before the gate, as a shield.
Redoubt—A small fortification completely closed by a parapet,
  thus allowing encircling fire.

Sally port—Exit for troops; fort entrance; gate.
Scarp—The front slope of the rampart or main wall of the fort.
Sponge—Brush or swab affixed to a pole and used for cleaning
  the bore of the cannon after discharge.
Tabby—(Sp. Tapia) A building concrete made from lime,
  shell, sand and water.
Terreplein—The horizontal surface in rear of the parapet, on
  which guns may be mounted.
Traverse—A barrier (as a bank of earth) across part of a
  defensive area, to give protection form enfilade fire.
Wormer—A double screw on the end of a pole, used for
  extracting the wad or cartridge from a muzzle-loading gun.

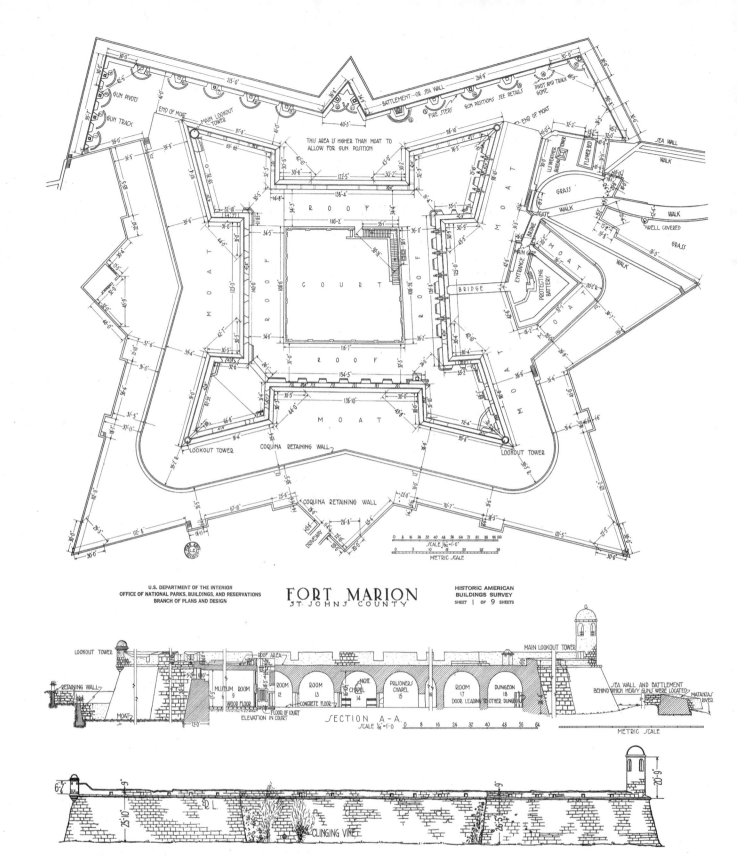

EAST ELEVATION

Bibliographical Note: This book THE HISTORY OF CASTILLO DE SAN MARCOS incorporates all of the text and most of the illustrations from *The Building of the Castillo de San Marcos* by Luis Arana and Albert Manucy, published by Eastern National in 1977. That publication was based mainly upon manuscripts in the *Spanish Records Collection of the North Carolina Division of Archives and History (Raleigh), the Stetson Collection in the University of Florida Library (Gainesville), the East Florida Papers and Woodbury Lowery's "Florida Manuscripts" in the Library of Congress (Washington, D.C.), and royal decrees in the Archivo General de la Nacion (México).* This publication has additional text by Jay Humphreys, layout and design by Henry Hird. Many of the historical maps are from *The Defenses of Spanish Florida* by Verne Chatelain in 1941. Other illustrations are from the St. Augustine Historical Society and the collection of Henry Hird. Color photos by John Cipriani and Henry Hird. *Learn more about St. Augustine by visiting* www.augustine.com